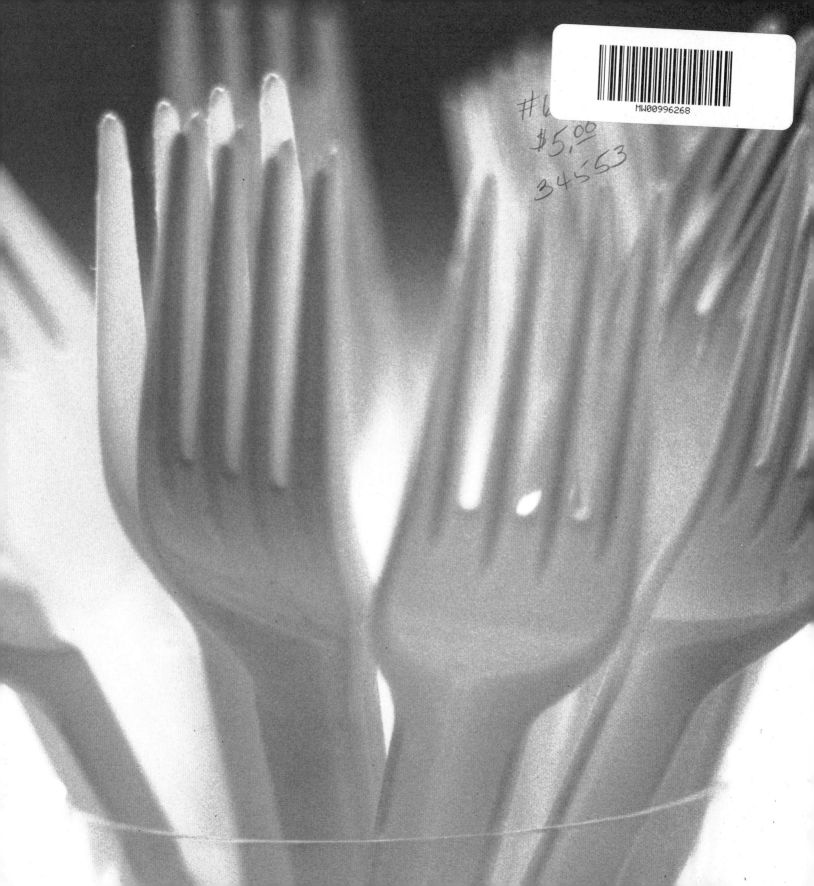

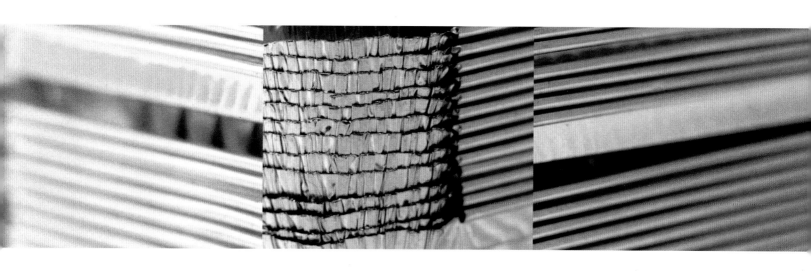

street food

street food

Clare Ferguson

photography by **Jeremy Hopley**

TIME®
LIFE
BOOKS

Alexandria, Virginia

Time-Life Books is a division of Time Life Inc.

TIME LIFE INC.

President and CEO: George Artandi

TIME-LIFE CUSTOM PUBLISHING

Vice President and Publisher   Terry Newell
Vice President of Sales
and Marketing   Neil Levin
Project Manager   Jennie Halfant
Director of Acquisitions   Jennifer Pearce
Director of Special Markets   Liz Ziehl

TIME-LIFE is a trademark of Time Warner Inc. U.S.A.

Books produced by Time-Life Custom Publishing are available at a special bulk

discount for promotional and premium use. Custom adaptations can also be created

to meet your specific marketing goals.

Call 1-800-323-5255.

Ferguson, Clare.

Street Food / Clare Ferguson : with photography by Jeremy Hopley

p. cm.

Includes index

ISBN 0-7370-0030-9

1. Cookery. International. 2. Snack foods. I. Title.

TX725.A1F418 1999

641.59--dc21   98-46942 CIP

First published in the United Kingdom in 1999 by Ryland Peters & Small,
Cavendish House, 51–55 Mortimer Street, London W1N 7TD.
Text copyright © Clare Ferguson 1999.
Design, photographs and illustrations copyright © Ryland Peters & Small 1999.

Printed and bound in China by Toppan Printing Co.

Dedication
To my husband, Ian, for encouraging these adventures in the first place.

Acknowledgments
My thanks to all those people in many parts of the world who have helped me with this book,
including Fiona Smith (assistant and recipe tester), designers Penny Stock and Sailesh Patel, editors
Elsa Petersen-Schepelern and Maddalena Bastianelli, indexer Hilary Bird, photographer Jeremy Hopley,
stylist Wei Tang, Catherine Brown, Sue and Martin Fish, Mikki Hariani, Sushu Kamlani, Sunil Vijayakar,
Violet Oon, Tony Lim of the Singapore Tourist Board, Patricia and David Galloway, Harlan Walker, Philip and
Medea Walker, Barrabel Mason, Alaphia Bidwell, Christine Boodle, Stella Shamwana, and Alex Austin.

■ **notes**
All spoon measurements are level unless otherwise noted.
Ovens should be preheated to the specified temperature. If using a convection oven,
adjust times and temperatures according to the manufacturer's instructions.

contents

introduction

Why do people eat exactly what they do?

There's a complex, hidden logic in it somewhere, composed of history and geography, trade patterns, intermarriage, royal decrees, politics, climatic change, invasion and conquest, sea currents, mechanical inventions, religion, medicine, and folklore. But eating and cooking are living arts. Dishes and food habits evolve or are introduced, move on, get remodeled, fade into other things, get rediscovered elsewhere, and start again. Street food in particular keeps a sort of gutsy honesty and authenticity, and it's possible to trace a certain pattern in its evolution. It's a sort of survival cuisine and in the same way is the truest food you'll ever taste. Fashion doesn't really touch it very much. It is real. Street food is a catchy melody played in many different harmonies and in minor as well as major keys.

Street food also implies energy and resourcefulness. Many people the world over may never be able to afford a seat in a plush indoor restaurant but still manage to eat superbly well. They assemble and share food in crowded alleys, in tree-shaded squares, under covered shopping malls, in ancient cobbled medinas, or under the faded silk canopies of temples. These scenes please us, reassure us and give us a sense of continuity. When I think back through some of my most vivid food memories, the ones I recall most affectionately are not the ten-course feasts in grand hotels or champagne and caviar tastings

with colleagues (though I'd never say no). Most often they are the unplanned, often chaotic but delicious snacks and drinks found at foreign bus stations and in far-off spice bazaars, in roadside diners or outside ferryboat terminals, at hawker stalls, in sun-streaked piazzas, in queues at fairgrounds, or on rickety verandas while waiting for the tropical rains to stop.

To our surprise these unlikely events often come out tops. Food and travel are happy bedmates. The foods, the situations are intriguing, often demanding, but rarely dull. Sometimes I find the thrill of recognition in a particular dish: a link to another place, another time, another recipe. But often not. Casual eating situations carry a particular cachet, it seems. So does the unique character of the raw materials, the novelty of the surroundings. Sounds also delight us: the sizzle of the outdoor barbecue, the sounds of the tuk-tuk drivers, the slap-slap of pasta being tossed from hand to hand.

Or it may be the particular proficiency of each street seller: the blasé ease with which each oyster is shucked, each dumpling sizzled, each flatbread filled and rolled and wrapped; the gush of sugar cane juice and ice into a glass, the roar of the flames in a tandoor as a baker detaches the hot bread and brings it out. What a wild gamble we take! Will it be as good as we hope, or better? Anticipation tends to give our hopes such marvelous savor! We get hungrier out of doors—a bonus. Adventures

Opposite, top row, from left **Mediterranean summer fruits are on sale from street fruit barrows all over Europe. Noodle maker in China. Bangkok's Floating Market.**
Second row, from left **Japanese child with a skewer of seafood. Beef cooking in bamboo steamers, Chengou, China. Woman mixing dough for turmeric-flavored crispbreads in a Delhi market.**

Third row, from left **Handkerchief-thin Egyptian flatbreads. Ice cream seller, Turkey. Pizza topped with spinach and pine nuts, Rome.**
Bottom row, from left **Fresh figs, peaches, and pistachios, bought from a Middle Eastern market in London. Italian ciabatta bread. Chopsticks—the perfect noodle-eating implement all over Asia.**

sharpen our appetites. Foods taste more distinct, textures crisper, colors are more intense, pungent smells drive us mad with optimism. Everything is more tantalizing altogether.

Street foods have been some of the minor joys of my life. Nothing pleases me more than being able to recreate that fun, that excitement, and verve in my own kitchen at home, for family and friends. With a beer, a cocktail, a vintage or two!

Informality promotes ease. Hand-held foods have a way of uniting all age-groups. Leaf-wraps intrigue guests. Sometimes I've found, in compiling these dishes, that one particular recipe is difficult to recreate, absolutely accurately, in spite of advice from locals, chefs, reference books, and my own experimentation. This doesn't seem to matter. One of the best aspects of street food for me is that it is so very durable, so adaptable, so opportunistic. So I invent, adapt, as they would do. But when I've found that my version, let's say, of staggeringly delicious Bombay *dosai* is just too difficult to do, is lacking the magic or simply doesn't taste good enough, I've ditched it—no apologies—and found another recipe which is more achievable. Better by far, I think, to return to that town, that country and enjoy the real thing, *in situ*, done to perfection, than a poor copy. And anyway, waiting makes appetites grow bolder. So this book contains some of my street vendors' best, my favorite treats from street markets all around the world. I am indebted to pancake-makers and bakers and barrow-owners and spice-sellers and confectioners, barmen and chefs, short-order cooks and waiters. Sometimes there is an account of when and how and why a particular was selected. Naturally, it is arbitrary and opinionated—this is, after all, my own collection of recipes.

There are regions I have yet to visit, new places to discover. Many of their dishes, therefore, may not feature here. Hopefully these will find their way into a further collection at another time. For countries such as India, where street food is such a consummate art and a revelation, there will seem a tiny sample: places like Nepal, Russia, Pakistan, or Cambodia barely get a mention. This is not to say that they lack wonderful local dishes—more that we just had to draw the line, somewhere, or perhaps I have not yet visited these countries. Europe, North America deserve a tome all to themselves: their street foods are so multi-cultural, varied, so diverse. So does Brazil. Not to mention the Caribbean. Southeast Asia,

Left **Squares of** *tortilla de patate* (Spanish potato omelet), **served with drinks in tapas bars.**
Opposite, above **Portuguese pastries;** *pasteis de nata* **and** *linguas de gato* (cat's tongues).
Opposite, below **Coffee and pastis liqueur, France.**

of course, is a wonderland of good street eating—Singapore, Bali, Thailand make our jaws drop in amazement. I have included as much as I could. China, particularly Hong Kong, is alive with food treasures to eat on the streets.

Memories come flooding back when I open these pages. One such memory is of being shown how properly to dismember a blue swimmer crab. I was crouched in a New Orleans hotel bathtub, wearing only a bikini—it was during a hot spell. The Creole maid who'd come to clean my bedroom couldn't resist tutoring me. We ate it, happily, together.

Then there was the time in Acapulco—fresh off the boat— when we devoured delicious tortillas filled with a succulent meat, then licked our lips, only to discover skinned bats strung up on the stall next to the one where we'd eaten. Hey—it tasted good! Never mind the consequences.

Or lost in the Plaka, Athens, one hot September. A bread-seller took pity. He handed me something wrapped in waxed and brown paper, as well as a luscious ripe peach. That gift turned out to be the best *bougatsa*—Greek custard pie—I'd ever tasted, and the best peach. The juice dribbled down my chin—I was content to remain lost there forever.

Another memory: a pyramid of scarlet crayfish on newspaper, in an outdoor parking lot in downtown Auckland, New Zealand. No lemons, no salt, no mayonnaise. Just cold beer. It was divine. The Samoan family traded me four crayfish in exchange for my London tube-map. A deal. Then there was that afternoon on Chowpatty Beach, Bombay. I awoke from a nap on the sand to find circus monkeys dancing, girl acrobats tight-rope walking, and the best mango *kulfi* ever on sale. Next came hot sweet cardamom tea. Pure pleasure.

Street food is basic, straightforward. It pulls no punches. Often you must use your eyes, nose, and your own discretion about whether it is safe to eat or not, and how much to pay. That is up to you: it is part of the challenge. Often the difficulty is in knowing when to stop. At home you have more control.

Initiative, creativity, verve, and energy typify many of my street food selections. These things are the factors that make street eating such fun. The chatter, clatter, the whistles, children tugging at your skirts, and the general enthusiasm also help. Hunger for excitement does the rest.

Here's to street food and all who make it possible. Enjoy these recipes: they come with some good memories.

Top row, from left Coffee—the ubiquitous street beverage from Seattle to Stockholm, Sydney to Sienna. Chinatown in New York is one of the city's major sources of exciting street food. Sandwiches are named after the Earl of Sandwich, who didn't have to stop gambling to eat them.

Second row, from left Hot dog stand, New York City: named after a popular canine cartoon character, hot dogs are the English-language version of a common European snack, known as *pölser* in Danish and *bratwurst* in German. Stacks of tortillas (corn flatbreads) on sale in Mexico.

Bottom row, from left Deep-fried ring doughnuts need nothing more than a coating of crunchy white sugar for a sweet treat at any time of the day. *Helados* (ice cream) vendor in Bolivia: ices, such as gelati in Italy, *kulfi* in India, and sorbets in France, are perfect street foods.

The many waves of immigrants to the New World of the Americas, combined with the intrinsic verve of its indigenous peoples and their superb, diverse local produce, has led to a colorful, eclectic food culture. Include, too, the energizing effects of African slave food traditions and brave new culinary technology and you get a dynamic, no-holds-barred street food tradition.

the americas

The Americas are a wonderland of raw materials, races, and traditions. Its foods and drinks form a veritable feast, with memorable street foods that have spread around the world. The first colonists, the Spaniards, Portuguese, British, and French brought new ingredients, while the cultural diversity was extended, reinforced, and enriched by slaves from Africa and the waves of Central European and Asian immigration in the nineteenth and twentieth centuries. These newcomers stubbornly hung on to the familiar dishes of their homelands and so embellished the American cooking lexicon.

In North America, industrial and technological advances improved the lot of many. Diets broadened. Incomes increased. Choices grew wider. People moved to the cities and there, out on the streets, along with the new affluence, electric lights, and state-organized hygiene, there appeared street-food vendors galore. Canning, dehydration, and the refrigeration of foods meant lively street snacks and ritual promenades.

Rushing to work, earlier and earlier, people grabbed an orange juice and a doughnut. Lunch became a hot or cold sandwich. At night, when people felt short of energy, or time, or both, they could pick up a hot dog or sausage, served from street stalls.

Fiestas, parades, bank holidays—whatever the occasion—to snack or "graze" in public had become fashionable and part of the American way of life. And now, when we ask a street vendor for lox and bagels, a hot dog, or a hamburger, or when we long for sushi, hanker after a *mojito*, or yearn for a danish, we are taking part in the continuation of the noble tradition of culinary integration that is part and parcel of North America. Conversely, these same foods have migrated around the world: you can eat pizza in Delhi or southern fried chicken in Islamabad.

But consider the other Americas. In Central and South America the Aztec, Carib, Mayan, and Arawak peoples were overwhelmed by Europeans, and with the conquistadores came Catholicism, hogs, horses, cattle, chickens, and goats, as well as changes in eating habits. In turn, the produce of these areas migrated around the world—chilies made an indelible mark on Asia, potatoes and tomatoes on Europe, and chocolate on appreciative female palates everywhere!

Though street foods of the region show influences from Europe, Africa, the Middle East, and Asia, indigenous dishes such as tortillas and barbecues have spread to every corner of the world. Mexico's variations on the tortilla seem endless—street stalls sell flour or corn tortillas with selections of fillings including chilies, cooked meats and poultry, refritos, guacamole, and sauces like adobos, recados, and salsas. Tamales (leaf-wrapped chopped meat or vegetables with masa dough) and empanadas (crispy filled pastries) are popular far from their native shores. The foods of the Caribbean are even more diverse—indigenous chilies and other ingredients influenced dishes introduced by slaves from Africa, workers from India, and plantation owners from Britain, Spain, France, and even Denmark. Rum is produced in infinite variety, and rum cocktails and other drinks are consumed with enthusiasm.

The street foods of South America are hugely diverse and as varied as the terrain. They range from the wonderful barbecued meat and corn of Argentina, Paraguay, and Uraguay, to the spicy dishes and ceviches of Peru and Ecuador, the Creole cooking of Guyana, French Guiana, and Surinam, the *arepas* (corn cakes) of Venezuela and Colombia, and the rabbit and potato dishes from Bolivia. My favorite South American street food area is Brazil, with its Indian, African, and Portuguese influences and delicious drinks such as *suco misto* or *batida*, based on its incomparable fruits and spirits.

hush puppies

Louisiana Cornmeal Fritters

I first tried these fritters, piled into a funnel of waxed paper, in the praline-scented back streets of the French Quarter in New Orleans, though they are commonly served as a side dish, especially with fried fish. According to tradition, they got their name because fishermen in the Louisiana bayous tossed them to their hounds to stop them jumping into the water and wolfing down the fish before it could be landed.

⅓ cup corn kernels (fresh, frozen, or canned)

½ cup all-purpose flour

1½ cups white or yellow cornmeal

2 teaspoons baking powder

½ teaspoon paprika

1 teaspoon salt

1 egg, beaten

1 cup buttermilk or thin plain yogurt

1 onion, grated

corn oil, for frying

Makes 20

Put the corn, flour, cornmeal, baking powder, paprika, and salt into a bowl and mix well.

Beat the egg and buttermilk or yogurt in a second bowl, then stir in the onion. Stir into the dry ingredients until just mixed—do not over-mix, or the hush puppies will be tough.

Fill a saucepan one-third full of corn oil or fill a deep-fryer to the recommended level. Heat the oil to 360°F or until a cube of bread browns in 40 seconds.

Scoop out large spoonfuls of the batter and drop gently into the hot oil. Cook till golden outside, and soft, steamy and damp inside—about 4 minutes. Serve plain, or with ketchup or chili sauce.

Mix the flour, baking powder, and salt in a bowl and make a well in the center. Stir in ¾ cup plus 2 tablespoons warm water, and mix to a dough.

Knead for 1–2 minutes until soft, not sticky, then divide into 4 balls. Roll or stretch each one to a 12-inch diameter circle, about ⅛ inch thick. Cut a 1-inch diameter hole in the middle of each one, so they cook evenly.

Fill a deep skillet or wok with 2 inches of oil or lard and heat until medium hot. To test the heat, drop the small circle of dough into the oil: it should sizzle and color gradually.

Slide one large circle of dough into the oil and cook for 1½ minutes, turn with tongs and cook 1½ minutes more. Remove and drain on crumpled paper towels.

Repeat until all the fry bread circles have been cooked, then serve them hot with your choice of toppings such as honey and cinnamon, jam, maple syrup, or tomato salsa.

1⅔ cups all-purpose flour, plus extra for shaping

1 teaspoon baking powder

1 teaspoon salt

peanut oil, corn oil, or lard, for deep-frying

To serve

your choice of honey and cinnamon, jam, maple syrup, or tomato salsa

Serves 4

fry bread

Navajo Deep-fried Crispbreads

I discovered this deep-fried crispbread while driving through Arizona toward Mexico. Groups of Navajo women were cooking sensational, huge, fry bread beside a parking lot. I had mine with honey and cinnamon, but there were other delicious options including jam, maple syrup, or tomato salsa.
The hole in the middle of the crisp is an ingenious idea—it allows the oil to bubble up through and cook the middle at the same rate as the outside.
This just has to be one of the world's great snack foods, and makes an utterly delicious, homemade alternative to storebought chips to serve at a party!

arepas

Yellow Corn Cakes with Fruit Batidas

In Colombia and Venezuela they rave about these corn cakes, eaten at street fairs, bars, and markets all over the country. Cheese, fresh chili, and sugar aren't essential, but I think they taste good. Arepa meal, also called masarepa, is a ready-cooked prepared food (flour made from very starchy cooked corn)—not to be confused with cornmeal, polenta, or hominy grits. Queso fresco is a fresh Mexican cheese—use mozzarella if you can't find it.

1½ cups fresh or frozen corn kernels (from 3 cobs)

1¼ cups yellow arepa meal (masarepa) or semolina

1¼ cups grated cheese, such as Mexican queso fresco or mozzarella

1¼ cups grated cheese, such as Monterey Jack

1 teaspoon baking powder

½ teaspoon salt

3 tablespoons superfine sugar

2 fresh serrano or jalapeño chilies, cored and chopped

6 tablespoons milk

corn oil, for brushing

Makes 18

Process the corn in a food processor until fine. Transfer to a bowl, then mix in the arepa meal or semolina, the two cheeses, baking powder, salt, sugar, and chilies. Mix the milk with 1 tablespoon hot water, stir into the flour mixture, and mix to a stiff dough. Divide into 18 portions, roll into balls, and flatten into patties about ½ inch thick.

Preheat a stove-top grill pan or skillet, brush with oil, add the arepas in batches, and cook over low to medium heat for 3 minutes on each side, until golden and crusty outside and soft inside.

Serve for breakfast or as a snack with strong black coffee, fresh fruit batida, or orange juice.

Fresh fruit batida:

Peel and pit (where necessary) your choice of tropical fruit such as mango, guava, melon, or papaya. Put through a juicer or purée in a blender. Add sugar syrup or alcohol to taste, plus crushed ice and mineral water if necessary.

Acaraje were African slave food, and versions can be traced all over the Caribbean, central and southern Africa, the southern states of the US, and Central and South America. These days the spicy fritters make great party food! Sometimes acaraje are baked, but this version is fried—a true street treatment. In Brazilian market towns, especially near the coast, brilliantly dressed women sell acaraje on trays. In other places the fritters may be stacked inside heated glass cases in bars, sold with drinks such as a juice or caipirinha—Brazil's delectable cocktail. Dende (palm) oil—deep orange with an earthy taste—may be hard to find, except in Afro-Caribbean markets, but you can substitute annatto oil or corn oil instead.

acaraje

Black-Eyed Pea and Shrimp Fritters

1 cup dried black-eyed peas, soaked 24 hours in
  cold water, changed once

½ onion, chopped

½ teaspoon salt

1 malagueta or bird's eye chili, chopped, or
  ¼ teaspoon hot chili sauce

16 cooked shrimp, peeled or unpeeled

Vatapa*

¼ cup hot milk

½ cup soft white fresh breadcrumbs

¼ cup dried shrimp, chopped

2 garlic cloves, chopped

¼ cup chopped roasted peanuts

1½ inches fresh ginger, grated

½ teaspoon hot chili sauce

2 cups peanut or corn oil

½ cup dende (palm) oil, annatto oil,
  or corn oil

Makes 16

Drain the peas, then cover with cold water. Rub them between your palms—the outer skins will float off into the water. Let settle, then skim off the floating skins with a slotted spoon. Drain the peas well, then grind or purée with the onion in two batches in a food-processor or grinder. Add the salt and chili or chili sauce and process again.

Put all the vatapa ingredients except the oil in a food processor and purée to a thick paste. Set aside. Heat the oil(s) in a medium-sized heavy skillet to 360°F. Using 2 oiled dessert spoons, scoop out disk shapes from the pea purée. With a teaspoon, dig out a hole in the center of each one. Spoon a heaped teaspoon of vatapa mixture into the hole and smooth it flat, then push 1 shrimp on top—this will help bond both mixes together.

Slide the finished acaraje into the oil and fry for 3–4 minutes, or until cooked through. Remove and drain on crumpled paper towels, then repeat with the remaining mixture. Keep the acaraje hot in the oven until ready to serve with fruit juice, cocktail, or ice-cold beer.

Caipirinha Rum and Lime Cocktail

Chop ½ lime and put in a glass with 1 tablespoon superfine sugar. Mash, press, and stir to make the juices run. Add 4 ice cubes and ¼ cup white rum, such as Brazilian cachaca. Stir and serve.

■ **note:** In some places the vatapa is not added until serving time. (Brazilian vatapa is a purée of cooked meat, chicken, fish, or shrimp mixed with coconut milk, peanuts, dende oil, and other flavorings.)

cheeseburgers

Hamburgers with Aged Monterey Jack

The history of the burger is intriguing. Three Americans claim the honor of its creation; in 1885, 15-year-old Charles Nagreen, of Seymour, Wisconsin, found that his fairground customers liked his butter-cooked ground beef but wanted it portable to eat on the run, so he sandwiched it between slices of bread. Frank Menches of Akron, Ohio, in 1892 is also quoted, as is Louis Cassen in New Haven, Connecticut, in 1900, and Delmonico's restaurant in New York had hamburger steak on the menu as early as 1836, selling for just 10 cents a serving. So the debate rages!

Sprinkle the bread with water, squeeze it dry, and crumble into a bowl. Add the grated onion, salt and pepper, thyme or marjoram, Worcestershire sauce, and ground beef. Mix well, divide into 4 portions and flatten into patties.

Heat the oil in a skillet, add the sliced onion, and sauté until softened and golden. Keep hot.

If using bagels or hamburger buns, cut them in half. If using a baguette, cut it in half lengthwise, then crosswise into 4. Toast or broil the bread, bagels, or buns, or char-grill them, cut side down, on a stove-top grill pan. Keep them hot while you prepare the other ingredients.

Cook the hamburgers on a preheated barbecue, stove-top grill pan, or skillet, or under a broiler until well browned and crusty outside and cooked right through.

Divide the onions between the bread or buns, add a hamburger to each one, then top with cheese. Broil until the cheese is softened and melting.

Add your choice of accompaniments, then close up and serve.

1 thick slice bread, crust removed

2 onions; 1 grated coarsely, 1 sliced crosswise

1 teaspoon salt

½ teaspoon freshly ground black pepper

2 teaspoons fresh thyme or marjoram leaves

2 tablespoons Worcestershire sauce or steak sauce

1 lb. lean ground beef

1 tablespoon virgin olive oil

1 French baguette loaf, cut crosswise into 4,
    4 hamburger buns, or 4 bagels

4 oz. aged Monterey Jack, sliced into strips

all-purpose flour, for shaping

To serve (optional)

your choice of: lettuce, sliced tomato, pickles,
    mayonnaise, ketchup, or coarsely crushed
    black peppercorns

Serves 4

Mexican street stalls are a riot of color, life, and activity, and the endless varieties of tortilla-wrapped foods, such as flautas, tacos, burritos, enchiladas, and so on, are irresistible. This casual modern version of these traditional wraps makes useful brunch and lunch foods or splendid late-night snacks for tequila-tipsy revelers— I first tasted them in Mexico City's Zona Rosa after a wonderful party. Make sure your refried bean mixture is thick and spicy—mash in chopped garlic, cook with extra oil, cumin, chili, salt, and oregano to make it substantial, spicy, and packed with flavor. Add the garnishes below, plus your favorite salsa, homemade or storebought if time is short.

To soften the tortillas, spray them with a little water, wrap in foil, and put in a preheated oven at 350°F for about 10–12 minutes until warm and pliable. Alternatively, wrap in parchment paper and microwave on high for 3–4 minutes, or wrap in foil and heat in a bamboo steamer over boiling water for 5–10 minutes.

Spread 2–3 tablespoons of the refried beans on each tortilla. Add the chopped chili, lettuce, cheese, olives, salsa, and cream, fold up the base of the tortilla, then fold over the 2 sides, like an envelope. Serve warm, with cherry tomatoes, cilantro, or chilies.

■ **note:** To make a fresh salsa, chop 4 scallions, some cilantro and mint leaves, 2 teaspoons sea salt flakes, and 8 whole allspice, crushed. Mix, chill, and use within 2 days.

8 corn or flour tortillas, 8 inches in diameter

2 cups hot refried beans (refritos)

2 teaspoons chopped fresh jalapeño or serrano chili

¼ head crisp lettuce, such as iceberg

1 cup coarsely grated Monterey Jack

¾ cup pitted olives, green or black

1 cup salsa (see note)

½ cup sour cream

8 cherry tomatoes, chopped (optional)

sprigs of cilantro (optional)

2 fresh red chilies, chopped (optional)

Makes 8

tacos

Flour Tortillas with Refried Beans

Frankfurters, which originated in Germany, became dogs in the USA because of a popular dog cartoon character with a sausage-shaped body. This favorite snack, invented by Texan Neil Fletcher in 1942, has traveled well—you find corn dogs on the streets of cities from New York to Seattle, Chicago to New Orleans, and everywhere in between. Children have taken corn dogs to their hearts and bolt them down with enthusiasm.

corn dogs

Corn-Battered Hot Dogs

10 frankfurters

flour, to coat

spicy mustard or ketchup, to serve

corn oil, for frying

Corn batter

¼ cup fine yellow cornmeal

½ cup all-purpose flour

¼ teaspoon salt

¼ teaspoon baking soda

½ cup buttermilk or thin plain yogurt

1 egg

Makes 10

Soak wooden skewers in water for 30 minutes. When ready to cook, push a skewer lengthwise down the middle of each frankfurter. Dust with flour.

To make the batter, mix the cornmeal, flour, salt, and baking soda in a bowl. Put the buttermilk or yogurt and egg in a second bowl, beat well, then stir into the dry ingredients until smooth.

Pour 2 inches depth of oil into a deep-fryer or heavy-bottomed saucepan and heat to 375°F, or until a cube of bread browns in 30 seconds.

Dip the frankfurters into the batter to coat, and shake off any excess. Add the corn dogs to the hot oil in batches of 4–5 and deep-fry for about 4 minutes or until golden brown. Remove and drain on crumpled paper towels. Repeat with the other corn dogs, then serve hot with a dip of spicy mustard or tomato ketchup.

pollo pibil

Chicken in Banana Leaves

Delicious, finger-food-style snacks like this are found in market towns all over the Yucatan. A *pib* is a Mexican earth oven: a pit is filled with fire-heated stones covered with wet leaves. The wrapped food is placed on top, then covered with more wet leaves and piles of earth: the heat is contained and the food cooks until tender. In Hawaii this earth oven is called an *imu* and the New Zealand Maoris know it as the *hangi*, and the whole performance is a community event. The method is fun, friendly, but time-consuming—this recipe is a domestic equivalent. Annatto is sold in Latin American stores and gourmet shops, but if it is hard to find, use turmeric or half the amount of saffron threads: not the same, but equally colorful and aromatic.

2 teaspoons ground annatto (see note)

2 teaspoons black peppercorns

1 teaspoon allspice berries

1 teaspoon dried oregano

1 teaspoon cumin seeds

5 garlic cloves, chopped

2 tablespoons orange juice

1 lb. boneless, skinless chicken breasts,
   cut into 28 equal pieces

banana leaves or foil, for wrapping

coarse sea salt flakes, for dipping

Makes 28: Serves 4–6

■ **note:** If grinding annatto seeds yourself (in an electric spice grinder), add a little salt first—the seeds are very hard, and salt helps to produce friction.

Put the annatto, peppercorns, allspice, oregano, and cumin in an electric spice grinder or mortar and pestle and grind to a powder. Add the garlic and grind to a paste. Mix with the orange juice. Pour into a shallow, non-metal container large enough to fit the chicken pieces in one layer.

Add the chicken, turn well to coat, and set aside to marinate for about 5 minutes.

Cut the banana leaves crosswise into 2-inch strips. Put a piece of chicken at the end of one strip and roll up, corner to corner, to make triangular packages. Secure with wooden toothpicks.

Steam in a layered steamer for 15 minutes, or microwave on high for 3 minutes for 6 pieces and 5 minutes for 12 pieces.

Alternatively, bake in a covered roasting pan in a preheated 350°F oven for 35 minutes, or until the chicken is tender.

To serve, unwrap the packages, dip the chicken in sea salt flakes, and eat with your fingers.

Variation:

The marinade can be boiled until reduced to a sticky glaze, then served with the chicken.

jerk pork

Jamaican Barbecued Pork with Herb Dumplings

This spicy barbecued pork is eaten with the fingers or with bread rolls or dumplings. Its distinctive flavor is allspice, also known as Jamaican pepper or pimento (not to be confused with pimiento, another name for pepper or chili). Traditionally, jerk pork is cooked over coals made from the wood of this native Jamaican allspice tree. Dispensed with lots of loud reggae music, laughter, and much goodwill, it makes a real treat at London's Notting Hill Carnival, but Jamaicans can eat it all year round. Lucky things!

Mix the ketchup, citrus juice, and soy sauce in a shallow, non-metal dish, then stir in the sugar, peppercorns, allspice, chili powder, lime zest, garlic, and salt. Add the pork and set aside for 1 hour. To make the herb dumplings, mix all the dry ingredients in a bowl, stir in ¾ cup water, then shape into balls using 2 dessert spoons. Fill a saucepan one-third full of corn oil and heat to 360°F or until a cube of bread browns in 40 seconds. Deep-fry until crispy outside and fluffy inside. Drain on crumpled paper towels.

Grill the pork over a hot fire for 2 minutes each side, or cook under a very hot broiler. Serve plain, or with dumplings or rolls—and a rum punch.

Jamaican Rum Punch

Mix 1½ cups golden rum, the juice of 8 limes, ½ cup sugar syrup, and ice to taste. Top with sliced lime if you like. Pour into 4 glasses and serve. Sugar syrup is made by boiling equal quantities of sugar and water together until the sugar dissolves, it can be kept in the refrigerator indefinitely.

¼ cup tomato ketchup

¼ cup fresh lime or lemon juice

2 tablespoons dark soy sauce

1 tablespoon brown sugar

1 teaspoon coarsely ground black peppercorns

1 teaspoon allspice berries, crushed

½ teaspoon chili powder

½ teaspoon grated lime zest

3 garlic cloves, finely chopped

1 teaspoon salt, or to taste

1½ lb. boneless pork loin, chops or steaks, patted dry with paper towels

soft bread rolls, to serve (optional)

Jamaican herb dumplings (optional)

1⅓ cups all-purpose flour

½ cup nonfat dry milk

1 teaspoon baking powder

½ teaspoon salt

¼ cup chopped parsley

corn oil, for frying

Serves 4

shrimp roti

Caribbean Flatbreads with Curry Shrimp

½ cup unbleached all-purpose flour

½ cup whole-wheat flour

¼ teaspoon salt

¼ cup milk

¼ cup melted butter or peanut oil

Curry shrimp

1 tablespoon red Thai curry paste

1 inch fresh ginger, finely sliced

4 scallions, chopped

1 cup canned coconut milk

4 oz. peeled shrimp, cooked or uncooked

2 tablespoons toasted unsweetened dried coconut

1 tablespoon chopped fresh cilantro

   or flat-leaf parsley

¼ teaspoon salt

Serves 4

Trinidad Rum Punch

Serve with this traditional recipe:

"One of sour (1 part lime juice),

Two of sweet (2 parts sugar syrup),

Three of strong (3 parts rum),

Four of weak (4 parts water)."

Add ice, stir, and sip. Lovely!

In Northern India, *roti* is the collective word for all breads, but both name and concept have migrated around the world, especially to the islands of the Caribbean, where the word now means the whole dish—the bread, plus the curry served with it.

In Trinidad, roti are sold from colorful stalls set out under the coconut palms during the day, or at night from lantern-lit kiosks beside the beach, with steel drum music as a background. Tourists and locals alike adore roti—perfect finger-food to eat ambling along the beach or on the way to school. If you're making this dish for a party, increase the quantity and serve the curry in small bowls, and pile the roti on plates for people to help themselves.

Alternatively, eat it warm, part-wrapped in a twist of foil, with a rum punch.

Mix the flours and salt in a bowl. Pour the milk into a large bowl and stir in 6 tablespoons lukewarm water. Add 1 tablespoon of the melted butter or oil, then mix in the flour gradually to form a soft dough. Gather the dough together into a ball in the bowl and knead for 2 minutes. Clean the bowl with the ball of dough as you go. Remove the dough, brush the bowl with oil, replace the dough, then turn it over so it is coated with oil on all sides. Transfer to a plastic bag and set aside for 1 hour.

When ready to cook, divide the dough into 4 balls. Roll one ball to a circle, 8 inches in diameter. Brush with melted butter and fold in half. Press down the curved edge to seal. Butter the top surface and fold in half again to form a triangle. Press the edges to seal. Roll out to a larger triangle with sides of approximately 8 inches. Repeat with the other balls of dough to form 4 roti.

Heat a stove-top grill pan or skillet and brush with melted butter or oil. Add 1 roti and cook for 4–5 minutes, turning several times, until aromatic, firm, and speckled with brown. Repeat with the remaining roti. As they are cooked, wrap in foil and keep them warm.

Heat a skillet, add the curry paste, ginger, scallions, and coconut milk. Cook uncovered for 5 minutes, then add the shrimp and coconut to thicken.

Heat through (5–8 minutes) then add herbs and salt to taste. Serve in a bowl with the roti beside.

Alternatively, spoon a quarter of the mixture on each roti, fold up, wrap in foil, and eat on the run.

europe

European street food is as varied as its climate,

and if you consider the legacy of its colonial

past, the waves of incoming refugees over

centuries, and the sociable traditions of the

passeggiata, the evening stroll around the

streets, you begin to understand its splendid

scope. From the eat-and-run tradition of the

Danish open sandwich, to the pizza and gelati

of Italy, there is a world of possibilities and a

celebration of integration and cultural diversity.

Europe's street foods possess a diversity which is daunting

but also breathtaking. However, in much of Europe—especially in the north—a sense of puritanism about eating in public prevailed for centuries: it was felt inappropriate. This certainly has something to do with religion, but is also the effect of climate. Though much of Europe has a temperate climate, the weather can still be chilly—not conducive to eating outside in the street.

Such prejudices died slowly, but popular cooking has opened the door to outdoor eating and Europe has adapted its traditional foods to the new way of life. The range of dishes is vast, the scale endless. As well as regional specialities such as *choucroute*, smoked eel, and *socca*, consider well-traveled street foods like pretzels, bagels, brioches, croissants, *shawarma, gelati, frites*, pizza, quiche, doughnuts, and waffles. Add tapas and churros and you have some idea of the wealth of possibilities.

Street foods now include the indigenous dishes of each country, plus foods imported from former colonies and from other European countries and from America.

England and the Netherlands have embraced change almost too eagerly. It is difficult nowadays to find good fish and chips in much of Britain, yet kebabs, calzone, pasta, Thai green curry, onion *bhajia*, or dim sum are easy to locate. In Holland an Indonesian *rijsttafel* is sometimes more common than salt herrings or *speculaas* cookies.

Once upon a time, even in Greek country towns you could buy spit-roasted lamb by the pound. Today, sadly, it's often easier to find croissants, quiche, or Danish pastries.

Even in Poland, popular Western snacks are overtaking traditional Warsaw favorites such as spicy, crisp, pickled, baby cucumbers served in oak leaves—often eaten with rye bread and white cheese at street corner stands.

The French eat less standing on the street than inside good bistros or brasseries. Paris, however is the exception: here *crêpes, tartines,* croissants, *frites,* and *croques monsieurs* meet Japanese sashimi and Moroccan *tajines*.

The one street food it is always proper to eat in the street is ice-cream, and Europe produces some of the world's great examples; *jordbær* (strawberry) ice-cream in Denmark, *gelati di limone* in Italy, and *sorbet à la framboise* (raspberries) in France—only America, Australia, New Zealand, and India produce ice-creams as good as this. From the huge diversity found in Europe, the following recipes are, hopefully, a tempting introduction to Continental street dishes.

Top row, from left Mussels are popular in many parts of Europe, but nowhere more so than Belgium where they are prepared in myriad ways. French cheese is, arguably, the best in the world and baguette with cheese and a glass of wine has been a popular lunch for Frenchmen everywhere. Ice-cream is a favorite all over Europe, from the gelaterias of Italy, to the ice-cream parlors of Scandinavia—this one is in Helsinki, Finland.
Second row, from left Crispy nut-flavored, twice-baked Italian biscotti served with a digestif and *doppio espresso*. Belgian beer is the perfect accompaniment for the traditional Brussels street food of shoestring "French" fries and mayonnaise. Clams and other shellfish are cooked on outdoor grills all around the Mediterranean.
Bottom row, from left Grilled sardines dusted with sea salt are sold in Spanish markets and Portugal's streetside *restos*. Bread is the basis of the most common of all European street foods—the sandwich—appearing as *smørrebrød* in Denmark, "sarnies" in Britain, and bruschetta in Italy. Paella—the Spanish dish of rice cooked with saffron, shrimp, mussels, and often meats like chicken or rabbit—is best cooked for a large number of people, as in this street market.

frites et mayo

Belgian Fries and Mayonnaise

Not French fries, but Belgian ones! Thin, crisply fried, shoestring potatoes with a dollop of thick mayonnaise are comfort foods of huge appeal the world over, but the idea originated in Belgium. It's alarmingly rich, but reassuringly good, like so many street food combinations. So save your diet for another month, or try the frites with another Belgian specialty, mussels.

2 lb. floury potatoes*

olive oil and peanut oil, mixed, for frying

sea salt and freshly ground black pepper

Mayonnaise

½ cup extra-virgin olive oil

½ cup virgin olive oil

½ cup grapeseed oil

2 egg yolks, at room temperature

2 teaspoons Dijon mustard

2 teaspoons fresh lemon juice

¼ teaspoon salt

Serves 4: Mayonnaise serves 8–12

■ **note:** Potatoes fall into two categories; waxy and floury. Floury potatoes are best for baking and frying, and are often labeled as such. They will produce a crisp exterior and a fluffy interior.

To make the mayonnaise, mix the oils together in a small pitcher. Put the egg yolks into a small to medium bowl with high sides and a curved base. Stir in the mustard and half the lemon juice. With the oil container in one hand and a wooden spoon, whisk, or electric whisk in the other, gradually drizzle in the oil, stirring or beating continuously until a thick glossy emulsion sauce forms. When all the oil has been added, taste and add the remaining lemon juice. Cover the mayonnaise and chill*.

To make the frites, cut the potatoes lengthwise into ⅛-inch slices, then cut the slices crosswise to make ⅛-inch matchsticks. Put into ice water. When ready to cook, drain and pat very dry on paper towels or a clean cloth.

Fill a saucepan or deep-fryer one-third full of oil, and heat to 375°F or until a cube of bread browns in 30 seconds. Half-fill a frying basket with the matchstick potatoes, lower into the oil, and cook until mid-brown, about 4 minutes. Remove and drain on crumpled paper towels. Repeat until all the potatoes have been cooked.

Skim and reheat the oil to the same temperature. Add the potatoes and cook a second time until very crisp, about 2 minutes. Remove, drain, and keep hot. Repeat until all are cooked. Sprinkle with salt and pepper and serve with a large spoonful of mayonnaise.

■ **note:** To make mayonnaise in a blender or food processor, put the egg yolks and 1 extra whole egg in the bowl, turn on the machine, and drop in the mustard and half the lemon juice. Gradually drizzle in all the oil, then taste and add the remaining lemon juice.

tortilla de patata

Potato, Onion, and Bell Pepper Omelet

4 tablespoons extra-virgin olive oil,
   preferably Spanish

1½ lb. potatoes, halved lengthwise and
   thickly sliced

2–3 Spanish onions, sliced (about 1 lb.)

1 red bell pepper, cored and diced (optional)

6 eggs

sea salt flakes and freshly ground black pepper

Serves 6–8

Heat 2 tablespoons of the oil in a large, heavy-bottomed skillet. Add the potatoes, onions, and bell pepper and sauté over medium heat for 25–30 minutes or until tender, covering the skillet for the last 10 minutes, stirring occasionally.

Put the eggs, salt, and pepper in a bowl and lightly beat with a fork. Using a slotted spoon, transfer the potato mixture into the bowl and stir briefly.

Add 1 tablespoon of the oil to the skillet and heat until very hot. Quickly pour in the egg and potato mixture and reduce the heat to medium. Leave the omelet to cook, undisturbed, until the base is deep golden and firm, about 5–6 minutes.

Slide out the omelet onto an oiled plate, then put the skillet upside down over the plate and quickly invert the two. Drizzle the last measure of oil down the sides of the skillet and under the omelet. Cook over high heat until firm and golden—about 5 minutes. Remove from the heat and slide the tortilla onto a serving plate.

Cool a little, then cut into cubes or wedges and eat while still warm.

In Spain, fragrant cubes of warm tortilla are the perfect street food and a classic component of tapas, the selection of freshly prepared foods every self-respecting bar offers its patrons. You can adapt this traditional dish to serve as party food—wedges rather than squares may be more convenient to hold. A glass of Spanish wine such as Rioja, beer, or chilled amontillado sherry would make a splendid accompaniment.

Italian street foods are fantastic, and the pizza is perhaps the most famous of all, having migrated around the world, to wherever Italians have settled. Native to Naples, the original and best is the Margherita. Some, such as the *pizza bianco* or white pizza given here, have a topping, not filling, of spinach, raisins, pine nuts, and good olive oil heaped on top. *Tarte de blettes*, so famous in Nice, is very similar. Pizza slices, crostini, or bruschetta are also topped with eggplant, artichoke, or porcini paste and shavings of Parmesan.

pizza al taglio

Pizza Slices with Spinach and Pine Nuts

1 package (2½ teaspoons) active dry yeast

2 cups unbleached all-purpose flour

½ teaspoon salt

4 tablespoons extra-virgin olive oil

Pizza topping

4 garlic cloves, finely sliced

1 tablespoon fresh rosemary (optional)

2 teaspoons salt crystals or flakes

Spinach topping

2 cups young spinach, washed

½ cup raisins

¼ cup pan-toasted pine nuts

2 tablespoons extra-virgin olive oil

salt and freshly ground black pepper

Serves 4

Put the yeast, flour, and salt into a food processor fitted with a plastic blade and pulse briefly to sift the dry ingredients. Add ¾ cup lukewarm water and 2 tablespoons of the oil all at once. Process in short bursts for 15 seconds, until a soft mass forms (not a ball).

Turn out and knead for 2 minutes by hand. Slam the dough down hard, to develop the gluten.

Put the dough in a clean, oiled bowl and turn it once to coat in oil. Enclose in a large plastic bag and let rise until doubled in size—about 4 hours.

Remove and punch down the dough with oiled hands. Roll it out into a longish rectangle, suitable for slices. Push dimples into the dough, scatter with the garlic, rosemary, salt, and the remaining 2 tablespoons olive oil. Put on a lightly oiled baking sheet. Preheat the oven to 475°F.

Meanwhile cook the still-wet spinach with the raisins and pine nuts until the spinach turns brilliant green and is just tender. Stir in the oil, salt, and pepper and reserve.

Bake the pizza dough for 20–30 minutes until brown and crusty. Remove from the oven and pile the spinach mixture on top. Slice into 4 and serve hot, warm, or cool.

Provençal Tart with Onions, Olives, and Anchovies

In summer, the food market in Nice is enchanting. Produce is piled high in rainbow-colored profusion on stalls set up under striped awnings. The scent of herbs, aniseed, garlic, fragrant melons, and peaches makes your mouth water. *La socca* and *pissaladière* are typical local street foods here, while in Mallorca they make a dish similar to this one, known as *coca*, referring to its open face. Make your *pissaladière* as small, individual ovals, or as one huge tart, to be shared. Please yourself. Bliss!

1 package (2½ teaspoons) active dry yeast

1 tablespoon sugar

1 tablespoon milk

1⅔ cups all-purpose flour

1 egg, beaten

1 tablespoon extra-virgin olive oil, plus extra
   for greasing

1 teaspoon salt

Toppings

¼ cup (2 oz.) canned or salted anchovies

4–5 large onions (about 2 lb.), sliced

1 fresh bouquet garni of fresh thyme, parsley,
   and bay leaf

4 tablespoons extra-virgin olive oil or butter

about 1 cup black Niçoise olives

Serves 4

Put the yeast, sugar, milk, ½ cup lukewarm water, and 1 tablespoon of the flour into a food processor fitted with a plastic blade. Leave for 5 minutes until frothy, or proceed immediately if using easy-blend yeast.

Add the egg, oil, salt, and half the flour. Pulse for 1 minute. Add the remaining flour and pulse until the dough forms a sticky ball.

Transfer the dough to a large oiled bowl, put into a plastic bag, and seal well. Set aside for 1–2 hours at room temperature, or overnight in the refrigerator until doubled in size.

Meanwhile, to make the topping, prepare the anchovies—if canned, halve them lengthwise: if salted, soak in warm water for 15 minutes, then drain, fillet, and halve the fillets as before.

Heat the oil in a large skillet, add the onions and herbs, and cook over low steady heat, until caramelized and sweet but not brown (about 30–40 minutes).

Preheat the oven to 450°F. Divide the dough into 4 and pat into ovals, plaiting the edge if preferred. Place on an oiled baking sheet, push dimples into the dough with your fingers, then bake for about 7 minutes.

Remove from the oven and cover the dough with onions, then add the anchovies in a criss-cross pattern, and put olives in between the diamonds. Return to the oven for 10–12 minutes. Serve hot.

pissaladière

Using an electric beater, blender, or food processor, beat the flour, salt, and 1 cup cold water to a creamy batter. Let stand for at least 10 minutes or up to 1 hour.

Heat a skillet until very hot and brush the surface with oil. Beat the batter again, adding a little extra water if necessary, to produce the consistency of thin cream.

Pour about ¼ cup of mixture over the pan—enough to make a thin coating. Cook over a high heat until the surface bubbles, the edges become crisp and golden, and the center is barely set—about 2–3 minutes. (It is cooked on only one side.)

Cut in half crosswise with a spatula, and fold each half in half again, making 2 wedges. Tip the wedges into a twist of paper or onto a plate, season with salt, pepper, or sugar and serve immediately. Repeat until all the batter is used (2 wedges make one serving).

1 cup besan (gram or chickpea flour)

1 teaspoon salt

virgin olive oil, for frying

salt, freshly ground pepper or sugar, to serve

Serves 4

la socca

Crispy Chickpea Pancake

■ **note:** Besan or gram flour is a pale yellow flour made from dried chickpeas. It can be found in Asian or Indian markets or at health food stores.

Typical Niçoise *socca* is a street food of great antiquity. It used to be the mid-morning snack for laborers, with vendors going from one building site to another, shouting their wares, but now everyone buys it from stalls in the street markets. It is cooked on a flat surface over fierce heat until the outer edges are frizzled but the center is still a little soft: it is kept warm over a brazier. Wedges are marked off and scooped up, outside to center, then scraped up like pleated fabric and served in paper cones, sprinkled with salt, pepper, or sugar. If making socca in an ordinary pan, 1–2 whole pancakes per serving should be enough.

fish supper

Scottish Fish and Chips

Fish and chips (called "fish supper" in Scotland) has been one of Britain's greatest exports. Crisp, flaky, freshly battered and fried fish—haddock in Scotland: cod in England—and plump, homemade french fries are cooked in beef drippings (an archaic method coming back into fashion) or good oil. They are then wrapped in newspaper and eaten in the street, on the quay, or carried home. Though there are many complex batter recipes, this extremely simple one is a favorite with many chippies (fish-and-chip shops). Typical accompaniments are brown sauce in Scotland, malt vinegar in England, or fresh lemon wedges in Australia and New Zealand—plus salt, pickled onions, or gherkins.

To make the batter, put the flour, salt, and beer or water in a medium bowl and beat until smooth. Drain the potato strips and pat dry with paper towels.

Melt the dripping or oil in a large, heavy-bottomed skillet to reach a depth of 1 inch. Heat to 400°F—use a frying thermometer to check.

Add half the potatoes to the skillet and fry them, turning several times with a spatula, for about 10–12 minutes. Remove, drain on crumpled paper towels, and keep hot in a moderate oven. Repeat with the remaining potatoes.

Divide the fish into 4 equal portions and pat dry on paper towels. Coat the pieces of fish in batter, turning them until well covered. Using tongs, put one portion at a time into the hot fat or oil. Cook until the batter is crisp and golden and the fish just opaque in the middle, about 3 minutes on each side (break one open with a fork to check).

Drain on crumpled paper towels and keep hot. Repeat with the remaining portions.

Serve on paper plates, or (traditionally) in butcher's paper and newspaper. Sprinkle with salt and pepper, followed by brown sauce or vinegar and serve with your choice of other accompaniments.

2 lb. floury potatoes, cut lengthwise then
   crosswise into ½-inch strips (keep in a bowl of
   ice water until ready to cook)
beef drippings or vegetable oil, for deep-frying
1½ lb. haddock or cod fillets, skinned
salt and pepper

Beer batter
1 cup all-purpose flour, sifted
1 teaspoon salt
1 cup flat beer or water

To serve (optional)
brown sauce, malt vinegar, or lemon wedges
pickled onions
gherkins

Serves 4

smørrebrød

Danish Open Sandwiches with Three Seafood Toppings

6 slices Danish light rye bread

6 slices pumpernickel

6 slices rye bread with caraway seeds

¼ cup unsalted butter

Trout topping

2 rainbow trout fillets, skinned

½ cup white wine vinegar

2 tablespoons sugar

2 tablespoons sea salt flakes

1 red onion, finely sliced into rings

6 cornichons (baby gherkins), sliced

Gravad lax topping

12 oz. fillet of wild salmon, about 6 inches long

⅓ cup sea salt flakes

¼ cup superfine sugar

¼ cup fresh dill, chopped

2 teaspoons crushed black peppercorns

6 fresh dill sprigs

Shrimp topping

36 cooked shrimp, peeled

12 chives or flat-leaf parsley sprigs

2 tablespoons mayonnaise

6 lemon wedges

Makes 18: Serves 6

Long before bruschetta and crostini became fashionable, the Danes had made the sandwich the height of easy culinary delight. A sunny Danish summer lunch has included food like this for generations—it's a home-style dish that has translated well to modern living, so it's become a popular takeout snack.

Denmark has the perfect raw materials for dishes like these: all Scandinavians set great store by good bread—in fact the bakery is the one shop that always stays open on Sunday—and the area is famous for its dairy produce, so the bread is always well buttered, not just because it's delicious, but to stop the bread becoming soggy under the weight of the gorgeous toppings. The seafood toppings listed below can be bought ready-made to save time, but marinated trout and homemade gravad lax are easy to do and taste terrific. Small versions of these sandwiches can be served as party food—and don't forget the traditional Danish drinks of good beer and aquavit (a usual chaser for cured fish dishes).

To make the trout topping, start the day before serving. Put the fillets in a non-metal dish about 2 inches deep. Heat the vinegar, sugar, and salt in a saucepan, stir to dissolve, then cool. Pour over the fillets, cover, and chill for 12–24 hours.

To make the gravad lax, rub the salmon all over with the salt, then the sugar, then pat on the chopped dill. Put the fish, skin side down, on a shallow, non-metal dish. Put a wooden board on top and press down. Add weight and chill for 24 hours.

Just before serving, butter the bread (this will seal as well as helping the toppings to stick).

Drain and slice the salmon, skin side down, cutting diagonally, to make 12–18 slices. Set several slices on each slice of rye bread. Add the pepper and a sprig of dill.

Drain the trout, pat dry with paper towels, and slice into wide diagonal strips. Put 2 on each slice of pumpernickel. Add red onion rings and cornichons.

Pile 6 shrimp onto each slice of caraway and rye bread. Add chives or parsley, a spoonful of mayonnaise, and a wedge of lemon.

Serve the prepared sandwiches on a board or large platter.

Although there is a trend in Greek *kafenions* and kiosks to sell non-authentic rectangular cheese pastries or *tiropittas* made from puff or flaky pastry, the real thing is worth seeking out. These are three-cornered, triangular pastries with cheese, egg, and herbs inside. They may be big (*tiropitta*) or small (*tiropitakia*). You can buy them hot, scented, and superb from the old traditional white-tiled bakeries which also sell other intriguing items like twice-baked bread (*paximathia*). Frozen phyllo pastry is now widely available at supermarkets. Work on one sheet of pastry at a time, covering the remainder with a damp cloth while you work—otherwise they dry out very quickly.

tiropitakia

Triangular Greek Pastries with Herbs and Cheese

6 sheets Greek filo pastry, about 3 oz.

¼ cup Greek extra-virgin olive oil

Cheese filling

8 oz. Greek feta cheese, crumbled

1 egg, beaten

2 teaspoons chopped fresh mint

1 teaspoon dried oregano or 4 teaspoons chopped
   fresh oregano

freshly ground black pepper

½ teaspoon ground nutmeg

Makes 18 large, 24 small: Serves 6

To prepare the filling, put the cheese, egg, herbs, pepper, and nutmeg in a bowl and mash to a paste. Chill until ready to use.

Put the pastry on the work surface and cover with a damp kitchen towel. Take 1 sheet of pastry, brush it with oil, then cut lengthwise with scissors into 3 strips (for *tiropitta*) or 4 (for *tiropitakia*). Put 1 heaped teaspoon of filling on the corner of one long strip of pastry. Turn one corner over toward the long edge. Continue folding over and over, corner to corner, to form a triangle, tucking any uneven ends underneath. Brush all over with oil and set aside on a baking sheet. Repeat until all the filling and pastry has been used.

Preheat the oven to 350°F, then bake for 20 minutes. Alternatively, deep-fry in batches in olive oil for about 1–2 minutes each side, then drain.

Serve hot, warm, or cold, and eat with your fingers. A cup of Greek coffee or a glass of retsina, ouzo, or Greek Fix beer would be a perfect, traditional accompaniments.

loukoumathes

Greek Fritters with Honey Syrup and Cinnamon

Put the yeast, flour, sugar, salt, and 1 cup lukewarm water in a bowl and mix well. Enclose in a plastic bag and leave in a warm place for 30 minutes to 2 hours, or until bubbling.

When ready to cook, take a handful of the stretchy, elastic dough. Squeeze it through the bottom of your fist and, with oiled finger and thumb of your other hand, pinch out small, walnut-sized pieces onto a plate. Alternatively, use 2 spoons, pincer-like, to pinch out blobs of the dough.

Fill a saucepan one-third full of oil and heat to 400°F—test with a frying thermometer. Drop the dough pieces into the hot oil and cook until a deep golden color, about 4–6 minutes in total. (Flip them over with tongs as they cook). Open one to test—the inside must be damply soft, not raw. Remove from the oil with tongs or a slotted spoon, drain on crumpled paper towels, and keep them hot while you cook the remainder.

To make the syrup, put the honey and lemon juice in a saucepan and heat until scented. Drizzle over the fritters and sprinkle with ground cinnamon.

In cafés, hole-in-the-wall snack shops, and street kiosks in Greece you'll sometimes see giant cauldrons of bubbling oil frying these fizzing doughnuts. I love them for breakfast, with a *metrio* (medium sweet coffee) in the afternoon, or as an outrageously delicious dessert, set out on a few fig leaves, and accompanied by thick, creamy Greek yogurt (they're also nice with crème fraîche). They're fun to make too—take a handful of the mixture, squeeze out a bubble of dough and pinch it off with the oiled thumb and forefinger of your opposite hand. The locals pinch it straight into the oil but do avoid scalding splashes: drop them in carefully.

1 package (2½ tablespoons) active dry yeast

2 cups all-purpose flour, sifted

1 teaspoon sugar

½ teaspoon salt

4 teaspoons ground cinnamon, to serve

corn or peanut oil, for deep-frying

Honey syrup

½ cup clear honey

juice of 1 lemon

Makes about 20

1¼ cups superfine sugar

1 cup whole milk

4 egg yolks

1 cup mascarpone or other cream cheese

Citrus flavoring

1 cup orange juice (about 4 oranges)

1 cup lemon juice (about 5 lemons)

1 cup clementine (mandarin) juice

(about 5 clementines)

1 tablespoon citrus liqueur

(limoncello or Cointreau)

½ teaspoon orange flower water

Strawberry flavoring

3 cups ripe fresh strawberries

1 tablespoon fruit liqueur or dark rum

½ teaspoon orange flower water

Makes 4 cups: Serves 8

To make the citrus flavoring, mix the juices, liqueur, and orange flower water, then strain.

To make the strawberry flavoring, put the berries in a bowl with ½ cup of the sugar and chop and mash to a pulp. Set the bowl in a saucepan of hot water for 10 minutes. Purée in a blender, then strain through a non-metal sieve and discard the seeds.

To make the gelato base, put the milk in a saucepan and bring to a boil. Put the egg yolks and remaining sugar in a non-metal, heatproof bowl, beat to a pale froth, then beat in the hot milk. Put the bowl over a saucepan of simmering water and stir gently until smoothly creamy and thick enough to coat the back of a spoon.

Fold in the mascarpone, about 1 tablespoon at a time, then stir until dissolved. Put the bowl in ice water to cool, stirring now and then. When cool, fold in the citrus juices or strawberry purée, as well as the liqueur and orange flower water. Stir until even.

Churn and serve immediately, or transfer to a plastic, lidded container and freeze. When ready to serve, soften in the refrigerator for 25–40 minutes before serving.

■ **note:** If you don't have an ice cream machine, pour the mixture into a lidded metal or plastic container and freeze for 4–6 hours, stirring the edges into the center every hour. The texture will be less creamy but it is still good.

italian gelati

Ice cream truly is the perfect street food. My favorites have always been French and Italian; honey-nougat ice cream in Provence, lavender and thyme ices in Nice, black currant sorbets flavored with crème de cassis, and the famous long queues outside Berthillon's in Paris for their vanilla, apple, peach, caramel, and rum-raisin. In the sun-streaked piazzas in Florence I've devoured gelati flavored with white peach, raspberry, marsala, and zabaglione. Sorrento, south of Naples, is one of the ice cream capitals of the world—and this *gelato di limone* reminds me of the wonderful ripe oranges and lemons tumbling over the high garden walls that overlook the blue Mediterranean. Strawberries are used to make a *gelato di fragole*, another classic ice cream. Serve gelati layered between cookies, in cones, or in glasses.

africa

and the middle east

From Turkey to Morocco and the Cape, from

Mozambique to Zanzibar, Middle Eastern and

African street foods have a vast and vivid scope.

They range from the imperial traditions of

Turkey to the Islamic-influenced foods of North

and West Africa, the European colonial

traditions of Southern Africa, and the Indian

influences found in East Africa.

Top Steaming mint tea is served in tea shops throughout Morocco. Tea shops are an all-male preserve in most of North Africa, but this modern iced version of traditional mint tea is a popular summertime drink for men and women in other parts of the world.
Left Fresh fruits such as figs and pomegranates are prized in all Arab and Arab-influenced countries, eaten fresh or dried. Figs taste particularly good with a sprinkle of pepper.
Below, from left Nuts are an important part of Arab and Persian cuisines, both raw, as here, and in cooked dishes. Huge handkerchief-thin flatbreads are used as eating utensils from Morocco through North Africa and the Middle East to Pakistan and Northern India. Women of Senegal making doughnuts for sale in the market.

Street foods in Africa and the Middle East have verve and distinctiveness. Expatriates, when talking about the foods of their homelands, often become very emotional, very sentimental, so passions and prejudices can make classification difficult. For the purposes of this book I regard Egypt, Syria, Turkey, the Lebanon, the Sudan, Jordan, Iraq, Iran, the Gulf States, Yemen, and Israel as part of the Middle East. Morocco, Tunisia, and Algeria I have classed as part of Africa.

Moroccan and Tunisian cuisines, with their fascinating Berber, Arab, and Spanish accents, are very fashionable in Europe and America, but other African foods are little known. So a paper twist of hot, spicy chickpeas or fava beans with salt and cumin are familiar, as are *kefta* (minced lamb kebabs), *harira*, or couscous. But Ghanaian *tatale* or joloffe chicken, or Zambia's *matumbuwa* (fat cook) doughnuts definitely are not.

In Africa, creativity makes for delicious, nutritious dishes using wheat, millet, corn, barley, rice, peanuts, and yams, as well as beans, peas, lentils, and plantains. In addition, flatbreads and soft dumplings, spiced nuts, plantain-based chips, peanut snacks, and melon seeds are typical street food. Romantic locations such as Zanzibar, Timbuktu, and Marrakech were once exotic outposts on the spice routes, so it's not surprising to find spicy *berbere, harissa, peri-peri,* and *chermoula* as part of the repertoire of spicy seasoning on offer in an African street market.

If Africa was the cradle of mankind, then the Middle East was the birthplace of all western civilization. Here, hospitality is an absolute. The richness and diversity is staggering, the influences wildly exotic. Today, in the hullabaloo of a Tel Aviv market, under cool palms deep in a shady oasis, against a white-painted wall in a cool medina, or on the canvas-draped market stall of an Arab trader set out beside the Arabian Sea there may be piles of spices, bean pastes, eggplants, cucumbers, baskets of dates or nuts, heaps of fruit, strings of chilies. The scope will be fascinating, the tastes stylish, opulent.

Here, luxury and poverty coexist. As you stroll along eating sesame-crisps, sipping *doogh*—a cool yogurt drink—or dipping lavash bread into a spiced vegetable stew and tucking it around sheep's milk cheese or succulent minced lamb with herbs, you are continuing an ancient habit of eating street food. Contrast this with a stylish feast of pressed caviar, on the Caspian Sea, with black rye bread and butter—not the usual sort of street food, but available if you know where to look.

Charcoal-cooked chestnuts and beets, halva, *sambusak* pastries, *kibbeh*, apricot syrups—what fascination these foods offer!

In Central and East Africa, snacks include sliced, grilled sweet potato, corn on the cob, *nswa* (deep-fried flying ants that I have on good authority taste like peanuts), nuts, and *biltong* (strips of dried meat). There are also influences from Arab and Indian cooking, especially from the western Indian states of Gujerat and Kerala, both of which have an ancient vegetarian tradition. The result is a rice-, lentil-, and vegetable-based cuisine with African influences in dishes such as plantain curry. Drinks sold freshly squeezed in markets are similar to those in other tropical countries: sugar cane, pineapple, and coconut water. Fresh and dried fruits such as dates are sold as snacks or for home consumption. This chapter contains some of the world's most intriguing tastes. Enjoy!

cig börek

Turkish Lamb Pies

16 sheets phyllo pastry or 8 large sheets, halved,

    or 1 quantity of pastry (see below)

sunflower oil, for brushing phyllo pastry and frying

Pastry

2 cups all-purpose flour, sifted

1 egg

1 tablespoon milk

1 teaspoon salt

Lamb filling

1 lb. ground lamb

1 onion, chopped

1 large tomato, peeled and chopped

1 teaspoon salt

1 teaspoon pepper

1 teaspoon ground cinnamon

a small bunch of flat-leaf parsley, chopped

Serves 8

Travelers returning from Istanbul wax lyrical about the spices, seafood, kebabs, succulent mint-scented lamb, layered nut pastries, desserts, and sticky candies. Most of all they love *böreks* filled with cheese or meat, sold hot in the street markets; they tell of market traders carrying trays on their heads towering with seeded breads, and the ancient guilds which still protect the food sellers. This is a country of fascinating contrasts: a blend of Western and Middle Eastern sophistication, yet with a peasant vitality and profound sense of hospitality. In Turkey this popular snack is made with *yufka* (a phyllo-like thin pastry) in sheets layered with oil. Make your own pastry to make semi-circle pies or use 16 phyllo sheets in place of the *yufka*, wrap each into a cigar shape, then deep-fry.

To make the filling, stir-fry the lamb, onion, tomato, salt, pepper, and cinnamon over high heat for 5 minutes. Add the parsley, remove from the heat, and let cool. Divide into 16 parts.

Pastry böreks Put the flour and salt in a bowl and make a well in the center. In a small bowl whisk together the egg, milk, and ½ cup of water, then add to the flour and mix to a soft dough. Turn out onto a lightly floured work surface and knead the dough for 2 minutes. Wrap in plastic and chill for 10 minutes. Divide the dough into 16 pieces and roll out to 5-inch circles. Put a portion of filling on one side of each pastry circle and brush the edges with a little water. Fold the pastry over the filling to make semi-circle pies and, using your finger or a fork, crimp the edges.

Phyllo böreks Put the phyllo on a work surface and cover with a damp cloth. Work on 1 sheet of phyllo at a time and keep the others covered. Brush the sheet with oil and spoon a portion of filling along half of one short end. Fold in the sides and roll up towards the end, to form a cylinder. Brush the end with oil and press to seal. Repeat with the other sheets of phyllo and the remaining filling until all the *böreks* have been made.

Heat the oil to 360°F or until a cube of bread browns in 40 seconds.

Deep-fry the pastry *böreks* in batches for 4 minutes or the phyllo *böreks* in batches for 3 minutes, turning them over with tongs halfway through cooking.

Drain on a rack, covered with crumpled paper towels, then eat hot.

Years ago, when I was on vacation in Tunisia, I fell in love with the intriguing mosaics of ancient Carthage and discovered mint tea and *ouarko* pastry—like phyllo but more elastic— sold outside the food markets. The vendors had trays set on their knees, piled high with circles of lace-fine, silky white pastry. These were then filled and cooked to form *briks*— wonderful street snacks. My favorite is egg with fish and spice. Quail eggs cook quickly and are the perfect size for *briks*—you'll find them in specialty shops and gourmet markets.

tunisian brik

Crisp Pastries with Spice, Fish, and Egg

6 oz. fish fillets, ground

¼ cup chopped fresh cilantro

¼ cup chopped fresh flat-leaf parsley

½ teaspoon salt

1 teaspoon cumin seeds

12 large sheets *ouarko* or phyllo pastry,

12 quails' eggs

peanut oil, for deep-frying

To serve

lemon wedges

harissa or hot spice paste

Makes 12: Serves 4

Mix the fish, cilantro, parsley, salt, and cumin in a bowl and divide into 12 portions.

Heat the oil in a wok, saucepan, or deep-fryer to 350°F while you assemble the *briks*, taking care not to overheat the oil. The *briks* need to be cooked as soon as they have been made.

To assemble the *briks*, fold 1 sheet of pastry in half, wetting the edges a little to seal. Add 1 portion of the fish mixture and make a hollow in the filling. Break 1 quail egg into the hollow. Fold the pastry in half once more, wetting the edges again to seal.

Form the pastry into a triangle, with the filling at the base. Twirl the pastry closed around the filling, pinching it around the "waist" to enclose securely. Repeat with the remaining pastry and filling until all the *briks* have been made.

Check that the oil is at the correct temperature—a cube of bread will brown in 40 seconds. Add the *briks* to the hot oil in batches and deep-fry for 1–1½ minutes or until golden and crisp. Traditionally, the yolks remain runny. For harder yolks, cook 1½–2 minutes.

Serve with wedges of lemon and a little harissa or other hot spicy paste for dipping.

loubia,

In Iran, a common street food treat is *labu*—whole beets roasted in coals. Served in wedges in a twist of newspaper, they embody comforting goodness. Another favorite is *loubia*—fava beans or flat beans cooked whole and scented with *gulpazh* (wild angelica). How exotic! These two are something rather different from the usual snack. If you are lucky enough to have a Middle Eastern or Iranian greengrocer at your disposal, ask him for the old-fashioned herb *gulpazh*. No luck? Substitute dried lovage (from herb shops or Indian stores)—not the same but also curious and good. Alternatively, if you have a garden, try growing ordinary angelica—once planted, it's virtually impossible to get rid of!

labu, and doogh

Angelica Beans, Roasted Beets, and Yogurt Doogh

Angelica beans

2 lb. fava beans, in the pods,
 runner beans, or flat beans

4 cups stock or water

¼ cup vinegar

2 tablespoons gulpazh (dried wild angelica)
 or dried lovage

Roasted beets

8 beets, raw and unpeeled, but well scrubbed
 (about 2 lb.)

salt and freshly ground pepper

lemon juice, to serve

Serves 8

To cook the beans, pull off and discard any strings. Put the whole beans, stock, and vinegar in a saucepan. Cook, covered, for 1¼–1½ hours for fava beans or 30 minutes for runner beans or flat beans. Drain and serve in bundles, wrapped in twists of paper or a cloth to keep them hot.

Put the beets on a grill rack over a low fire. Turn them gradually as each side wrinkles, darkens, and cooks. Keep turning until all sides are done, about 1½ hours. Use paper towels to protect your fingers as you pull off the charred black skin.

Serve the beets chopped or sliced, wrapped in parchment paper, sprinkled with salt and pepper, drizzled with oil, and a little freshly squeezed lemon juice.

Yogurt Doogh

Cool yogurt drinks like this are incredibly refreshing: in some parts of the world they are salted, in other places sweetened. To make *doogh*, beat 2 cups plain yogurt (preferably with live culture) with 1 cup ice water and 1 teaspoon salt or sugar until smooth. Pour into 8 small chilled glasses and serve, sprinkled with cumin seeds.

falafel

Fava Bean and Chickpea Fritters

Before war all but destroyed it, Beirut was the pearl of the Levant—alive with nightlife, seething with color, music, neon, commerce, vitality. Architecture boomed, shops burst with luxury goods, bars with exotic drinks, street stalls with all kinds of goods. It was a confident, thriving, sophisticated, cosmopolitan mix of cultures and cuisines.
This dish, a typical Lebanese street snack, is today found all over the Middle East, from Damascus to Jerusalem, from Marrakech to Alexandria. There are countless versions—this one is delicious, sustaining, and worth adding to your repertoire, as is the accompanying tarator sauce, made from tahini paste.

Soak the fava beans and chickpeas separately in lots of cold water, for 24 hours (or pour over boiling water, stir, and leave for 4 hours).

When ready to prepare, drain the beans and peas, put into a food processor, and purée, in short bursts, to a coarse paste. With the motor running, add, in batches, the scallions, garlic, parsley, cilantro, chili powder, cumin, coriander seeds, salt, and baking powder.

Scoop out walnut-sized spoonfuls of mixture, and press between your palms into saucer-shaped disks. Continue until all the mixture has been used.

Fill a saucepan one-third full with the oil and heat to 350°F or until a cube of bread will brown in 40 seconds. Add the fritters, 8 at a time, and deep-fry for about 1½ minutes, turning them over halfway through. Remove from the oil with tongs or a slotted spoon, drain on crumpled paper towels, and keep hot in the oven until ready to serve.

To make the *tarator bi tahini*, put all the ingredients in a blender with ⅔ cup hot water and blend to a creamy sauce, adding extra water if too thick. Let cool.

Slit open the warmed flatbreads, push 6 hot fritters into each one, add your choice of salad ingredients and a drizzle of dressing, then serve.

1¼ cups skinned dried fava beans

⅔ cup dried chickpeas (garbanzos)

8 scallions, chopped

4 garlic cloves, chopped

¾ cup chopped parsley

¾ cup chopped cilantro

½ teaspoon chili powder

2 teaspoons cumin seeds, crushed

2 teaspoons coriander seeds, crushed

1 teaspoon salt

2 teaspoons baking powder

virgin olive oil, for deep-frying

Tarator bi tahini (tahini sauce)

½ cup tahini (toasted sesame seed paste)

juice of 2 lemons

4 garlic cloves, chopped

salt and freshly ground pepper

To serve

6 khoubiz (flatbreads) or pita breads

Lebanese salad (a mixture of sliced lettuce, onion, tomato, cucumber, and radish)

Makes 36: Serves 6

4 flatbreads, such as pita breads, warmed

virgin olive oil, for dipping

Dukkah mix

⅔ cup sesame seeds

½ cup hazelnuts

½ cup roasted chickpeas*

½ cup coriander seeds

3 tablespoons cumin seeds

1 teaspoon dried thyme

1 teaspoon salt

½ teaspoon black peppercorns

2 tablespoons mild paprika (optional)

Makes about 3 cups: Serves 8

Think of a lively Cairo market—full of heady scents, vivid colors, with shimmering heat haze and lots of shouting. There's non-stop chatter and laughter, a cacophony of blaring car horns, children plucking at your skirts, market traders exhorting you try their products. I remember a man in a hooded burnous leaning against a fruit stall, dipping a piece of flatbread into oil then into a curious speckly brown mixture—*dukkah*, the poor man's dinner or the playboy's snack, and perfect travel food. Serve with *labneh* (balls of soft cheese), herbs, pickled chilies, sliced tomatoes, or radishes. Good? It's delicious! Keep some in your pantry.

dukkah

Nutty Spice Mix with Flatbread with Olive Oil

*Available from health food stores and Indian and Middle Eastern grocers.

Toast the sesame seeds in a dry skillet until golden. Roast the hazelnuts and chickpeas in the same hot pan for about 4–5 minutes or until aromatic. Remove and set aside. Reserve 2 tablespoons of the roasted chickpeas.

Pan-toast the coriander seeds and cumin until they darken, then let cool. Mix all the *dukkah* ingredients, except the paprika and reserved chickpeas, in a bowl, then grind in an electric spice grinder or mortar and pestle. Stir in the paprika and reserved chickpeas and serve with a separate bowl of olive oil. Torn flatbread is dipped first into the oil, then into the *dukkah*.

kibbeh

Lamb and Bulgar Wheat Patties

1 lb. twice-ground lamb (leg or shoulder)

1 cup fine or medium bulgar wheat or bourghul

1 onion, thinly sliced

½ teaspoon sea salt flakes

½ teaspoon coarsely crushed peppercorns

¼ teaspoon ground allspice

½ teaspoon ground cinnamon

½ teaspoon ground cumin

6 tablespoons finely chopped parsley (optional)

virgin olive oil, for shaping

To serve

Your choice of:

20 crisp lettuce leaves, salad , yogurt dressing (optional)

warmed lavash, pita bread, or other flatbreads

Makes 20: Serves 4

When I tasted *kibbeh* for the first time (with some trepidation), they were raw—a mixture of ground raw meat, bulgar wheat, herbs, and spices. The next time, they were hot and cooked. Both styles are delicious. The key point is to use good lamb, with a little fat, but no connective tissue. Have your butcher trim it carefully and grind it two or three times. In Turkey this dish is sold in nests of long crisp romaine lettuce leaves. In the Lebanon and Syria it is often cooked and served with a yogurt dressing, salad, and warmed pita bread.

Put the ground lamb in a large clean bowl, cover, and chill.

Put the bulgar into a second bowl and pour in 2 cups near-boiling water. Stir, then leave to swell and soften for about 30 minutes. Rinse the bulgar in cold water and drain in a sieve.

Add the bulgar and onion to the lamb and mix well with your hands. Add the salt, pepper, spices, and parsley. Knead the mixture well with oiled hands. Pat into 20 ovals or cylinders.

If eating raw, set one inside each lettuce leaf and serve. Alternatively, soak 20 wooden skewers in water for 30 minutes. Wrap the mixture around each stick, in long, thin sausage shapes, leaving a "handle" of skewer at the end. To cook, fill a saucepan one-third full with oil, add the kibbeh, 5 at a time, with the sticks resting against the rim of the pan, and deep-fry for 2 minutes each until golden on the outside and rare in the center. Serve hot with your choice of accompaniments.

■ **note:** Grilling does not give such good results.

2 tablespoons salted butter, chilled and diced

1 cup all-purpose flour

a pinch of salt

2 tablespoons sugar

2 teaspoons caraway seeds

1 teaspoon finely grated orange zest

1 egg, beaten

peanut oil, for deep-frying

Makes 20: Serves 4

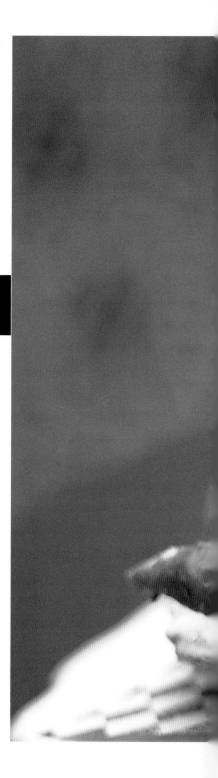

These popular crisp pastries are sold by vendors from trays or by stallholders near crossroads, bus and rail stations in Nigeria. They are fun, delicious, and pretty—and the kind of food that brings tears of nostalgia to the eyes of Africans living in other parts of the world.

chin chin

Crisp Caraway Twists

Cut or rub the butter into the flour and salt until it looks like coarse breadcrumbs. Add the sugar, seeds, and zest. Stir in the egg to make a stiff pastry.

Using your hands, gather the dough into a ball and knead for about 2 minutes. Roll out the dough to about ⅛ inch thick, cut into 1-inch wide strips, then 6-inch long strips, with angle-cut ends. Cut a slit at one end. Pull the other end through and tie it in a loose half-bow.

Fill a saucepan one-third full of peanut oil, heat to 350–375°F or until a piece of the rolled dough turns golden in 1 minute. Fry until crisp and golden, turning them once, using a slotted spoon or tongs, about 1–2 minutes. Remove, drain on crumpled paper towels, then eat immediately. Dust with extra sugar if preferred.

india

India is beautiful, huge, paradoxical. It seethes

with energy and vitality and has brilliantly

hospitable food traditions. Huge religious, racial,

tribal, and caste differences translate into a vast

street food culture that's endlessly delicious.

Barrows and streetside tea shops provide drinks,

fresh fruit, spice-sprinkled raw vegetables, and

cooked food non-stop from dawn to dusk.

India never fails to amaze. It is an exciting, dazzling, contradictory, and earthy country, with an elegance and spirituality which seem to be a natural part of the nation's psyche. Its foods are, in short, a wonder, and its street foods particularly are a celebration of human ingenuity.

The country is a glittering kaleidoscope of languages, dialects, faiths, castes, and traditions. Food, drink, and religious ritual are interwoven, with the ancient health code of the Ayurveda exerting a strong influence on the food of the eighty-five percent who are Hindus. Vegetarianism, rather than stifling cooking creativity, seems to help it thrive. In India, vegetarians eat superbly: never in my whole life have I so enjoyed subtle, pungent, spicy, balanced flavors, and matched textures than in the streets of Bombay. They fired my imagination. They were a revelation.

Street foods are of great importance to all Indians: even the richest bankers will send out for them. The *dabbahs* (tea shops) in every street provide an endless procession of naan and other flatbreads to accompany snacks and drinks like cooling lime sodas, or different kinds of tea such as sweet, milky *chai* or the elegant, cardamom-flavored green tea of the northwest. Also on sale are samosas (triangular, spicy, potato-filled pastries), onion and potato *bhajia* (deep-fried fritters), coconut-scented *dosai* (large, lacy pancakes), avial (vegetables cooked in coconut sauce), and crunchy, spicy "Bombay mix" (*sev* and *bhel puri*)—they all make wonderful street nibbles.

The beautiful southwestern coasts of Goa and Kerala produce superb street foods of great diversity, exciting to eat, especially on feast days when people take to the streets in a riot of color and fun. In temple-strewn Tamil Nadu, the street food is spicy, hotter, more intense, and often served on a banana leaf. Roasted spices sizzled in hot oil are sometimes poured on top. Peanut salads, *idlis* (small savory puff cakes), *appams* (pancake-like rice breads), *dosai,* and coffee are favorites.

West Bengal and its capital Calcutta teem with cultural energy and intellectual and political controversy— tea shop patrons, as in Paris, solve the problems of the world in conversation fueled by an endless supply of cakes and pastries. *Jalebi, sandesh, rasgullah,* and *payesh* are popular and also sold in pastry shops. High-heat tandoor clay ovens are found in *dabbahs*, restaurants, and bus stations across the country, but especially in the north. They produce skewers of meat, fish, or chicken, plus hot, delicious flatbreads such as naan, *paratha,* and *bhatura*—all treats for travelers and passers-by.

In short, India is a wonderland of good eating. Its many-textured food tradition is splendid, astonishing, and very regional. Eating and drinking is an astounding and valid way of learning to appreciate this fascinating, complex land. Its street food is a world all of its own.

Left Pappadams, the deep-fried crispbreads eaten as a snack throughout India, make perfect party food.

Top row, from left *Sev* and *bhel puri*, also known as "Bombay mix," are popular crunchy snacks. *Dosai* are lacy, crisp pancakes made of fermented rice and lentils, quick-fried on a huge cast-iron pan known as a *tawa*, like a shallow, upturned wok: *dosai* are often filled with spicy potatoes, or served with subtly flavored dips.

Center, from left *Jalebi*, a sweet, sticky, deep-fried pastry much-loved by Indians, who have a fierce sweet tooth.

Tea shop drinking vessels were formerly made of clay and broken after one use in the interests of purity and hygiene: metal containers are now common throughout India, and in this tea house in Nepal. Indian beers are often named after birds and animals; Kingfisher, Cobra, and Golden Eagle are just three—all are light, fizzy, and very satisfying with spicy food in a steamy climate.

Right Though most street foods are cooked and sold by men in India, this Gujerati woman is cleaning rice, removing small stones and twigs before cooking.

81

Samosas never meant much to me until I had eaten them, home-cooked, at a party given by a friend from Goa, the former Portuguese colony on the west coast of India, much visited by European beach-lovers. His mother's version uses fresh cilantro and cardamom in the potato filling: very good indeed. This dough is made with all-purpose flour, but sometimes besan (gram or chickpea flour) is used, and sometimes a mixture. This street food makes me want to visit Goa very soon!

samosas

Spicy Potato Pastries

Dough

3¾ cups all-purpose flour

1½ teaspoons salt

6 tablespoons ghee or clarified butter, melted

peanut oil, for deep-frying

sweet chili sauce, to serve

Spicy potato filling

¼ cup ghee or oil, heated

½ teaspoon cumin seeds, crushed

black seeds from 6 crushed green cardamom pods

3 potatoes, about 1 lb., cut into ½-inch cubes

4 garlic cloves, chopped

½ teaspoon ground turmeric

1 teaspoon salt

1 cup shelled green peas

6 tablespoons chopped fresh cilantro

Makes 24: Serves 8

To make the filling, heat the ghee or oil in a skillet and sauté the cumin and cardamom seeds until aromatic, but do not let them scorch. Add the potatoes and garlic and sauté for several minutes, stirring now and then. Add the turmeric, salt, peas, and ¼ cup water. Stir again, cover the skillet, and cook for about 10 minutes, until the potatoes are firm but tender, and the liquid has been absorbed. Uncover, then stir in the chopped cilantro and let cool.

To make the dough, sift the flour and salt into a bowl, then stir in the ghee. Add ½ cup plus 1 tablespoon hot water gradually, tossing and stirring, to make a dough. Knead for 2 minutes, then chill in the refrigerator for at least 25 minutes.

Divide the dough into 8, then roll or pat into 7-inch disks. Cut each disk in half, then form each semi-circle into a cone, overlapping and roughening the two edges, then wetting them to seal. Fill with 1 heaped teaspoon of filling. Wet the top and and pinch it closed, crimping neatly. Chill the finished samosa and continue until all are made.

Fill a wok or saucepan one-third full of oil, then heat it until very hot—350°F or until a cube of bread browns in 40 seconds. Add 3 samosas at a time and deep-fry until golden, blistered and crisp, about 3–4 minutes, turning them over halfway through cooking. Remove with tongs or a slotted spoon and drain on crumpled paper towels. Keep hot while you cook the remaining samosas. Serve with the sweet chili sauce.

In Bombay (now known by its original Maharashtran name of Mumbai), I ate *sev* and *bhel puri* at both ends of the catering scale—in the Sea Lounge of the elegant Taj Mahal Hotel, and then on the sands of bustling Chowpatty Beach, crammed with families and people selling everything under the sun. In between, I wandered through Colaba market, a buzzing chaotic bazaar, and ate authentic onion and potato *bhajia* for the first time, drank cumin-scented lassi and bought newspaper cones of the dried cereal-herb mix sold on every street corner by the *bhelwallah* (bhel-seller). Happy memories! This recipe helps recreate, in part, those flavors. Ideally you need a sev-maker, but you might like to try my alternative.

sev and bhel puri

Crispy Noodles and Rice with Salad

To make the *sev*, mix the besan, asafoetida, turmeric, cayenne, and salt in a bowl. Beat the oil and water in a pitcher, then drizzle gradually into the dry ingredients, mixing and kneading to make a soft, sticky dough. Divide into 3 portions, cover, and chill for 20 minutes.

Fill a wok or saucepan one-third full of peanut oil and heat to 350°F or until a cube of bread browns in 30 seconds. Using a sev-maker or coarse grater, force walnut-sized balls of the first portion of dough through the holes, firmly and slowly, to make thin noodles.

Move the whole apparatus in a circle as you do it so that the noodles fall in a curling stream. Fry for 30 seconds, remove with a slotted spoon, then drain on crumpled paper towels. Continue until all the dough has been cooked, then cool well. Next, roll pea-sized balls of the second portion of dough, deep-fry for 3 minutes, then drain. Roll similar sized balls of the third portion and flatten into 2-inch disks. Prick all over with a fork, deep-fry for 3 minutes, then drain.

For an instant snack, toss together all the *bhel puri* salad ingredients, except the rice. Heat a dry skillet until very hot. Add the rice and heat, shaking it, until it pops and becomes crispy and brown. Cool and add to the *sev* mix.

Serve separate bowls of all the different *sev*, salad, and your choice of chutneys. Provide spoons so people can mix their own just before eating, otherwise the sev become soggy.

Sev masala

3 cups besan (gram or chickpea flour)

½ teaspoon asafoetida powder

½ teaspoon ground turmeric

2 teaspoons cayenne pepper

2½ teaspoons salt

½ cup peanut oil, plus extra, for frying

Bhel puri

6 fresh green and red chilies, finely sliced

1 cup chopped fresh cilantro

2 scallions, finely sliced

1 small red onion, halved and sliced

1 teaspoon seasoned salt

2 tablespoons lime or lemon juice

⅓ cup long grain rice

Serves 8

1⅓ cups semolina

1 teaspoon salt

¼ teaspoon baking soda

½ teaspoon baking powder

1 cup plain yogurt

1 teaspoon black mustard seeds

2 tablespoons canned coconut cream

vegetable oil, for greasing

Coconut chutney

7 oz. fresh coconut, in chunks

1 green chili, chopped

3 garlic cloves, chopped

1 inch fresh ginger, sliced

½ teaspoon salt

black seeds from 12 green cardamom pods

1 cup canned thick coconut milk

1 teaspoon corn oil

2 tablespoons yellow split peas (channa dhaal)*

¼ teaspoon black gram (urid dhaal or black lentils)*

¼ teaspoon black mustard seeds

¼ dried chili, crushed

4 fresh curry leaves (optional)*

a pinch of asafoetida

Makes 20: Serves 4

■ **note:** Sold in health food and Asian stores.

Idlis are a passion with Indians, especially in the vegetarian south. Eaten for breakfast or as snacks from street stalls, they are usually made with fermented ground rice, and can be difficult for Westerners to make at home. This recipe, created by Linley Scott, uses semolina instead, and is easy to make, pale, pretty, and delicious when accompanied by a spicy coconut chutney. *Idlis* look like little flying saucers, and can be made at home using the tiered metal *Idli* "trees" sold in Asian hardware stores, or in oiled cups or small heatproof bowls. On street stalls, you often see them being made in large metal cupboard-style steamers, with clouds of steam billowing out whenever the doors are opened.

idlis

Puff Cakes with Chutney and Yogurt Lassi

To make the coconut chutney, peel the brown skin off the coconut with a vegetable peeler. Put the coconut, chili, garlic, ginger, salt, and cardamom seeds in a food processor and blend until fine. Add the coconut milk and blend again. Heat the oil in a skillet, add the two dhaals, mustard seeds, chili, curry leaves, if using, and asafoetida. Stir until the seeds pop and the mixture smells aromatic. Stir into the coconut mixture and serve.

To make the *idlis*, put the semolina, salt, baking soda, baking powder, and yogurt in a bowl, beat well, then let the mixture rest for 30 minutes. Stir in the mustard seeds, coconut cream (from the unstirred top of the can), and 4–6 tablespoons water.

Oil 20 *idli* molds or large muffin pans. Put 1½ tablespoons of batter into each one. Steam for 10 minutes—no longer or they may overcook, discolor, and spoil in flavor. Serve warm or cool with the coconut chutney and a sweet or savory yogurt lassi.

Indian Lassi

Put one part plain yogurt in a blender with one part milk, two parts ice, and 1 teaspoon sugar or ½ teaspoon salt per serving. Add other flavorings such as cumin seeds, crushed fruit, or freshly chopped mint. Blend and serve in tall glasses.

tandoori murgh

Tandoori Chicken

2½ lb. chicken legs, skinned, then

    slashed diagonally 4 times

2 teaspoons mild paprika

2 teaspoon sea salt flakes

1½ cups plain yogurt

2 teaspoons hot red chili powder

2 inches fresh ginger, grated

2 garlic cloves, crushed

black seeds from 12 crushed green cardamom pods

a large pinch of saffron powder (optional)

1 teaspoon cumin seeds, crushed

1 inch cinnamon stick, crushed

½ teaspoon cloves, crushed

2 tablespoons vinegar or lime juice

¼ cup ghee or clarified butter, melted

1 lime, in wedges, or 6 mint sprigs, to serve

Serves 6

Although now almost a cliché, this recipe is a well-known and well-loved Indian dish. It originated in the Northwest Frontier Province of what is now Pakistan, and has spread throughout North India and to Indian restaurants around the world. Though there are countless superb chicken dishes served as street food all over the Subcontinent, this one is a favorite. Of course a tandoor oven is not available to most of us, so this fast-cooked approximation is a good alternative. Color is important in Indian cooking—yellow and red are particularly prized. However, try to use vivid red chili powder—Kashmiri chili is ideal— and avoid lurid dyes or the so-called tandoori spice mixes containing red pigment. Serve this chicken with fresh mint, lime pickle or spicy chutney, pilau rice, or a soft fragrant bread.

Dry the chicken well with paper towels. Rub the paprika and salt into the slashes and all over the surfaces. Mix the yogurt in a bowl with the chili, ginger, and garlic.

Put the cardamom, saffron if using, cumin, cinnamon, and cloves in an electric spice grinder and grind to a powder. Stir into the yogurt marinade.

Dip the chicken into the marinade until well coated, then chill for 30 minutes, or up to 24 hours. When ready to cook, preheat a heavy baking sheet at 400°F for 10 minutes, brush it with ghee or clarified butter, and heat until melted. Add the chicken and drizzle with the remaining ghee or butter. Cook in the upper third of the oven for 30–40 minutes, depending on the size of the chicken legs. Pierce with the point of a sharp knife: the juices should run clear yellow. If not, cook a little longer. Remove from the oven and serve hot, warm, or cold with your choice of accompaniments.

kabob jhinga

Char-Grilled Spiced Shrimp

In beach-side shacks and street-side restaurants in the beautiful state of Goa, on the west coast of India, this superb dish is a popular snack. The size of Goan shrimp is jaw-droppingly impressive, but you should use whatever large shrimp are available: tiger shrimp, jumbo shrimp: even smallish lobsters or crayfish.
The *masala* (spice mix) is different from cook to cook, and area to area in India, but often includes black pepper, black cumin, cinnamon, cloves, mace, cardamom, bay leaf, and, ideally, famous Kashmiri red chilies, which give an intense red color and pungency. It is always better when the spices are freshly ground—see the suggested combination below.

Soak 8 wooden or bamboo skewers in water for about 30 minutes.

Slash the curved backs of the shrimp, then remove and discard any black threads. Pat the shrimp dry with paper towels. Grind the paprika, dried chilies, garam masala, turmeric, coriander seeds, and salt with a mortar and pestle or spice grinder. Add the ginger and garlic, then grind to a rough powdery paste. Add the ghee or butter and juice of one of the limes. Stir well. Rub the mixture into the shrimp, pushing it under the shells so it penetrates the flesh.

Thread 2 shrimp onto each skewer, then broil or grill over a low fire until aromatic: the flesh should be white and firm and the shells pink. Serve with the remaining lime, cut in wedges.

■ **note**: To make *garam masala*, mix 2 tablespoons each of crushed cinnamon, cumin seeds, and coriander seeds in a small skillet. Add 1 tablespoon each of the seeds from green cardamom pods, peppercorns, cloves, and ground mace. Dry-toast to release the aromas, then cool, grind in a spice grinder, and either use immediately or store in a jar with a tight lid.

2¼ lb. large uncooked tiger shrimp, shell-on

(about 16)

Spice mix

2 tablespoons mild or hot paprika

1 teaspoon kashmiri dried chilies, crushed

¼ cup garam masala*

2 teaspoons ground turmeric

1 teaspoons coriander seeds, crushed

1 tablespoon sea salt flakes

2 inches fresh ginger, grated

4 garlic cloves, crushed

½ cup ghee or clarified butter, melted

2 limes

Makes 8: Serves 4

Indian *kulfi* is a dense, rich ice cream, made by boiling down and reducing milk, then sweetening. India's favorite Alphonso mangoes are superbly fragrant and delicious. They, with orange flower water and cardamom, make this recipe very memorable. No fresh mango available? Use drained, canned mango if you must—good but less aromatic. This recipe is easy, but takes lots of time. If you don't have time, substitute 3 cups evaporated milk and ½ cup dried milk powder instead—the results are excellent.

mango kulfi

Indian Mango Ice Cream

Pour the milk into a large, wide, heavy-bottomed saucepan and bring to a boil, stirring often. Use a heat diffuser, if possible, to prevent scorching. Simmer, stirring every 15 minutes, for 3–4 hours or until the volume has reduced to about 3 cups and the milk is thick and dense.

Stir in the sugar, then cool the pan and its contents in ice water. Stir in the mango flesh, orange flower water, and cardamom seeds.

Put into a blender and purée, in batches, until smooth. Stir well, pour into ramekins, cups, or *kulfi* molds and fast-freeze for 4 or 5 hours or until firm. When ready to unmold, transfer to the refrigerator for 20 minutes, or dip briefly in cool water.

To serve them the Indian way, cut a deep cross in the top of the turned-out *kulfi*, so they thaw evenly. Serve, sprinkled with chopped pistachios and almonds, if using.

2 quarts milk

¾ cup sugar

4 cups diced fresh ripe Alphonso mango flesh

1 teaspoon orange flower water

black seeds from 20 green cardamom pods

finely chopped pistachios and almonds, to serve
  (optional)

Makes 1½ quarts: Serves 8

south
east asia

Street food in Southeast Asia—Thailand,

Vietnam, Malaysia, Indonesia, the Philippines,

Singapore, Burma, Laos, and Cambodia—is

among the very best in the world, with noodles,

satays, and other foods flavored with chilies,

lime, coconut, lemongrass, and soy or fish sauce.

Top row, from left Bundles of fresh lemongrass. A boatload of watermelons in Bangkok's Floating Market.
Center, from left Singapore shopping basket overflowing with Chinese flowering chives. Vietnamese women in the old imperial city of Hue on their way to the market, carrying baskets and pots of food on their cycle rickshaw. Coconuts on the island of Bali, Indonesia.
Right Street trader in Hoi-an, Vietnam, on her way to work.

The real excitement of eating in any of the countries of Southeast Asia is on the streets. Somehow eating al fresco like this evokes a nostalgia for brighter, more carefree days, for holidays, celebrations, feasts, and festivals and the joy of mildly disapproved-of pleasures in the slightly puritan West.

In this part of the world, foods made and consumed in public places carry no such stigma. Snacks enjoyed on street corners, by canals, in fairgrounds, parks, and parking lots have absolute significance and become an everyday event though they are never taken for granted. There is a passion for unearthing the most pungent pickle, the most scented mango, the sweetest pancake, the silkiest dumpling, the best bean paste, the most succulent satay, the most tempting brochette, the crispiest noodles, the freshest bread.

But to begin to describe the street foods of Southeast Asia at all—that immense, diverse, and intriguing area of the globe where public eating becomes an artform—is almost impossible. To try to sum it all up in just a few paragraphs is nonsense.

Even so, for people like you and me who wish to cook some of its better-known delicacies and learn a little about its great street food traditions, even a small attempt is worthwhile.

Southeast Asia includes Malaysia, Indonesia, Singapore, Thailand, Burma, Laos, Cambodia, Vietnam, and the Philippines. These countries contain a fascinating diversity of races, religions, cultures, traditions, and cuisines. In spite of exchange between these peoples along with influences from the West, and in spite of advances in agriculture and technology, a most distinctive character can still be seen and tasted. A unique charm in the everyday food of each country is still apparent, and none more so than in street fare.

In some ways street foods are survival dishes: they are able to tap into a vanishing past which has become blurred by the pressures and restrictions of life in the big city.

So, when you step out of your air-conditioned train, plane, bus, or ship into the brilliant, vivid, noisy, sultry, scented, congested kaleidoscope of sensations which is Southeast Asia, you feel almost shocked by the sweetness of the assault. Intense tastes, delicate textures, vividly contrasting smells, daring combinations, and inexplicable sounds as food is prepared—a vast repertoire of spiciness, sweetness, saltiness, bitterness, and savoriness. Under temple canopies, silk awnings, canvas tents, cotton umbrellas, wide-spreading trees, neon-lit verandas, and sheltered terraces, local people display their wares. Many will be prepared dishes, some will be local fruits and vegetables. But because street foods frequently have to be displayed, cooked, and sold without the benefit of refrigeration, the turnover must be rapid, the heat of cooking intense, the spicing and pickling often concentrated as a way of preserving foods and safeguarding flavors. Freshly cooked dishes do offer some degree of safety—and some delicious possibilities into the bargain. We Westerners have much to learn: the recipes in this book are just a few of my favorites.

On any street corner in Vietnam, in among the parked bicycles, you'll see people devouring bowls of steaming noodle soup—a national institution. The raw materials are lined up at the ready; great cauldrons of hot stock, piles of glistening white fresh rice noodles, heaps of green aromatics, and woks sizzling with beef, chicken, or pork. The stock is made from beef bones, ginger, salt, and garlic. When all their flavor has been extracted, these are strained out. Aromatics such as star anise, cassia, fish sauce, and roasted onions are then added, together with a large chunk of beef brisket that is cooked until tender. If this method is impossible for you, use any good beef broth, then add the flavorings. Herbs, beansprouts, and sauces are added to taste by each customer—Asian basil, with its purple stems and aniseed scent, is best for this dish, but any pungent mint can be used.

pho bo

Vietnamese Beef and Noodle Soup

2 oz. dried rice stick noodles

1 lb. fresh wide rice noodles*

12 oz. sirloin or bottom round steak, finely sliced

4 scallions, finely sliced

¼ cup chopped fresh cilantro

4 small red onions, finely sliced

3 quarts boiling beef stock (see introduction)

To serve

4 lime wedges

a bunch of Asian basil or fresh mint

a bunch of cilantro leaves

2 cups beansprouts

hoisin sauce (optional)

chilli sauce (optional)

Serves 4

Soak the dried rice sticks in hot water for 15 minutes. Drain, rinse, and drain again. Dip the fresh rice noodles into boiling water for 35–45 seconds: they must not overcook, but be properly heated right through. Drain, then divide all the noodles between 4 deep soup bowls. Add the sliced beef, scallions, cilantro, and onions.

Pour over the boiling stock and serve with china soup spoons, chopsticks, and small bowls of lime wedges, basil or mint, cilantro, beansprouts, and the sauces, all of which are added to taste.

■ **note:** If no fresh rice noodles can be found, increase the dried noodles to about 10 oz. Soak, drain, rinse, and use as described above.

loempia na carne

Philippine Pork Spring Rolls

2 tablespoons peanut oil

8 oz. pork tenderloin, finely sliced

1 small onion, finely sliced

4 garlic cloves, sliced

1 inch fresh ginger, grated

2 small hot red chilies, chopped

2 carrots, grated

⅛ small cabbage, finely sliced

1 teaspoon ground turmeric

12 lumpia wrappers (or spring roll wrappers)

4 teaspoons all-purpose flour mixed with ¼ cup water, for sealing

peanut oil, for frying

Chili dipping sauce

½ cup rice vinegar

2 garlic cloves, chopped

1 hot red or green chili, sliced

salt and freshly crushed black pepper

Serves 6

Heat the oil in a skillet, add the pork, onion, garlic, ginger, and chilies, and sauté until aromatic and the pork is no longer pink. Stir in the carrot, cabbage, and turmeric. Cover and cook for 2–3 minutes. Remove from the heat, let cool, then divide into 12 portions.

Detach each lumpia wrapper from the pile. Put 1 portion of filling on each wrapper, near a front corner. Fold in the side flaps to cover it then roll up like a parcel, sealing the ends with a little flour and water paste.

Fill a saucepan or wok one-third full of the oil and heat to 360°F or until a piece of noodle will puff up immediately. Add the lumpia, 4 at a time, and deep-fry until golden, crisp, and well cooked through, about 3–4 minutes. Remove and drain on crumpled paper towels. Mix the chili dipping sauce ingredients in a small bowl and serve with the lumpia, either whole or cut in half diagonally.

Wrapped foods, part of an ancient heritage, are very much in demand all over the world. Delicious, colorful *loempia* or lumpia—the Philippine version of the ubiquitous Asian spring roll—are part of this tradition. In Manila's street markets, with their huge piles of tropical herbs, spices, fruit, and amazing vegetables, they are piled on leaf-covered wicker trays with bowls of dipping sauce. Square or round spring roll or lumpia wrappers are sold, vacuum-packed, in refrigerator cases in ethnic stores or Asian grocers. They may need to be pried apart—the vacuum effect makes them stick together.

Satays are some of the most famous street foods in Southeast Asia: on every fifth corner, you'll see *gerais* filled with satay sticks, radiating out like colorful fans. Try to find authentic ingredients (a Chinese grocer will have all these ingredients), or use fish sauce or anchovy paste instead of blachan; if no tamarind, use lemon juice; if no lemongrass, use lemon zest. If you don't have time to make the spice paste, use green Thai curry paste thinned with lime juice and a little oil.

chicken satays

1 lb. boneless chicken breast, skinned

2 tablespoons peanut oil

2 tablespoons distilled white malt vinegar

Spice paste

3 garlic cloves, chopped

4 shallots, chopped

1 tablespoon coriander seeds, crushed

2 teaspoons cumin seeds, crushed

½ stalk lemongrass, finely chopped

1 teaspoon ground turmeric

2 small, fresh hot red chilies, finely chopped

Satay sauce

1 teaspoon blachan (shrimp paste), toasted on a
    piece of foil for 1 minute (or use fish sauce)

1 teaspoon tamarind paste (sold in jars)

1 oz. macadamia nuts or peanuts, chopped

1 tablespoon palm sugar or brown sugar

½ stalk lemongrass, finely sliced

4 shallots, chopped

2 small, fresh hot red chilies, chopped

½ cup canned coconut milk

Makes 8: Serves 4

Cut the chicken breasts into 1-inch cubes or thin ribbons. Put the pieces into a non-metal bowl. Grind the spice paste ingredients together in an electric spice grinder. Heat the oil, add the spice paste, and sauté until aromatic. Cool, stir in the vinegar, then add to the chicken. Marinate for about 20 minutes or up to 2 hours. Meanwhile soak 8 wooden satay sticks in water.

To make the satay sauce, put the toasted blachan or fish sauce in a blender, add the tamarind paste, macadamia nuts or peanuts, sugar, lemongrass, shallots, and chilies. Heat the coconut milk in a small saucepan to near-boiling point, then add to the blender, and purée briefly to form a sauce. Light a grill or preheat a broiler until very hot.

Push the meat onto the sticks—if using ribbons, thread them on in waves—then grill or broil or cook on a stove-top grill pan for about 3 minutes on each side. Serve with the satay sauce.

otak otak

Fish in Banana Leaf Parcels

Singapore should be called snack city—the choice is just endless. Its Nonya or Peranakan dishes are famously delicious—a fascinating combination of Chinese and Malay traditions. Singapore's famous food dynamo, Violet Oon, has taught me how to make many intriguing recipes, including these fish quenelles. Instead of being poached in the European way, they are wrapped in banana leaves and grilled over charcoal, giving a delicious fragrance. Later, exploring the markets, I often saw these charred green parcels for sale. They are succulent, superb, easy to carry and eat with your hands—ideal street food. *Otak otak* can be eaten as they are, or with dipping sauces or chunks of lime or lemon.

The drinks were terrific too: I was particularly impressed by one made with rose-flavored evaporated milk—luridly pink, in string-tied plastic bags with straws—which was very good. I also loved the Asian favorite—fresh, green coconut with the top lopped off and a straw for sipping the cool, scented coconut water.

Put the fish into a large bowl. Add the lime leaves, salt, and sugar, stir, and let stand. Cover the chilies in hot water and soak for 20 minutes or until softened. Drain and put in a large mortar or an electric food-processor. Add the ginger, turmeric, shallots, cilantro, lemongrass, nuts, and blachan (shrimp paste). Work to a purée.

Heat 3 tablespoons of the oil in a wok, add the spice paste, and stir-fry until aromatic. Cool slightly, add it to the fish mixture. Stir in the coconut milk. Knead until smooth. Cut the banana leaves or foil into 6-inch squares, rub them with the remaining oil, and spread 2 tablespoons of filling along the front side, parallel to the ridges if using banana leaves. Fold over and over. Pin the ends closed with short wooden skewers. Repeat to make 20 parcels. Light a grill or preheat the oven to 450°F. Cook the parcels over a hot fire or in the oven. Remove when they smell aromatic and feel set and firm. Serve still wrapped; unwrap and eat on the spot.

■ **note:** Alternatively, cook, 10 at a time in a circle in an 850 watt microwave. Microwave on HIGH for 2 minutes. Turn them over and reposition after 1 minute.

1¼ lb. boneless white fish fillets, such as cod, skinned and ground

8 kaffir lime leaves, very finely sliced

1½ teaspoons salt

¼ cup sugar

20 small dried red chilies

2 inches fresh ginger, peeled and finely chopped

1 tablespoon ground turmeric

12 shallots, finely sliced

1 tablespoon coriander seeds, pan-toasted then crushed

1 stalk lemongrass, finely sliced

4 candlenuts or macadamia nuts, or 6 cashews, chopped

1 tablespoon blachan (shrimp paste) or fish sauce

1 egg, beaten

1½ cups thick canned coconut milk

4 tablespoons corn or peanut oil

2 lb. fresh banana leaves, wiped with a wet cloth, (alternatively, use foil)

Serves 4

tod man

Thai Spicy Fish Cakes

These tiny, tasty, bite-sized fish cakes are an everyday item and perfect for finger food occasions. They are an essential taste of Thailand, yet have now traveled all over Europe and America and are currently a craze in many trendy cafés and restaurants. Use whatever fish you like: white fish is usual, but I prefer these made with salmon or trout—all are good. Do try to locate fresh kaffir lime leaves: frozen will do, but never dried—they will never give the same delicious fresh taste. A razor-sharp blade or scissors will slice them best: they must be hair-like, utterly thin. If you can't find them, the grated or finely sliced zest of two limes could be used instead. Thai cooks use yard-long beans, but baby asparagus is easier to find. Remember Thais use the roots and stalks of cilantro, as well as the leaves, so try to buy the herb intact. Galangal is a spicy-sweet rhizome related to ginger: it is superb, but not essential—ordinary fresh ginger can be used instead.

Put the fish, shallots, ginger or galangal, lemongrass, cilantro, garlic, lime leaves, sugar, and fish sauce or soy sauce in a non-metal dish and marinate for 30 minutes for flavors to mix well.

Transfer to a food processor and work to a coarse mixture: do not reduce to a paste. Stir in the sliced asparagus, salt, and pepper.

Shape the mixture into 42 small balls, flatten into ½-inch thick cakes, and season well. Heat a stove-top grill pan or skillet and brush with oil. Add the fish cakes in batches and cook 1–1½ minutes on each side, or until golden and cooked right through. Serve with chili sauce or lime wedges.

2 lb. fish, such as salmon or trout, skinned, boned, and cubed

8 shallots or small red onions

2 inches fresh ginger or galangal, finely chopped (optional)

1 stalk lemongrass, finely sliced

4 cilantro roots including stems and leaves, chopped, or ¾ cup chopped leaves

4 garlic cloves, chopped

4 kaffir lime leaves, sliced hair-thin

1 tablespoon sugar

1 tablespoon fish sauce or soy sauce

8 oz. thin asparagus, finely sliced

salt and freshly ground black pepper

peanut oil, for brushing

chili sauce or lime wedges, to serve

Makes 42: Serves 6

2 cups milk

1 cup sugar

2 cups unsweetened, canned coconut milk

1 tablespoon dark rum or fresh lime juice

thin strips of lime zest or lime wedges, to serve

Serves 8

A friend of mine spent part of her childhood in Burma and, along with mangoes and sticky rice, she remembers coconut ice cream as one of the most treasured tastes of that time. I have tried to recreate these memories for her in this superb, easy recipe, based on an original by chef Douglas Rodriquez of Patria in New York. Though the rum is definitely not Burmese, it tastes wonderful.

coconut ice

Burmese Coconut Ice Cream

Put half the milk and all the sugar in a heavy-bottomed saucepan and bring to a boil, stirring until dissolved. Remove from heat. Add the remaining milk and the coconut milk. Cool the mixture over ice water and stir in the rum or fresh lime juice.

Transfer to an ice cream maker and churn for 25–40 minutes, or according to the manufacturer's instructions, until firm and silky.

Alternatively, freeze in plastic trays until the mixture is hard at the edges but soft in the center. Remove and stir well, then refreeze as before. Repeat and refreeze.

Serve in bowls, glasses, or cones, topped with lime zest, or with lime wedges for squeezing.

cream

The ancient traditions underpinning street food in China, Japan, and Korea succeed in giving it freshness, beauty, and huge taste appeal. Eating in the chaotic, busy marketplaces of all three countries is an education in itself: the considered selection of perfect ingredients, their cutting, combining, and cooking over a fierce flame, is taken to a high art.

china
japan and korea

To eat authentic food in homes or restaurants

in China, Japan, and Korea is a revelation. But to eat good market food dishes, in the streets, honestly prepared, while all around trolleys clank, hawkers bawl, voices babble, woks clatter, and flames hiss and sizzle, is a daily miracle of life there. Fresher than fresh is the ideal—and often the reality. Fish is filleted before your eyes, radish grated, and batter poured to order—it's just like a spectator sport.

Fundamentally, Chinese food is very simple, elemental. Stir-frying is perhaps the best-known aspect of their cooking, but crisply deep-fried delicacies, steamed dim sum, and buns matter much more. It is these foods that are easily tackled with the fingers and that can be bought on the street served in paper, plastic, on leaves, or in cardboard boxes. The Chinese have always been great travelers and have migrated to almost every country in the world. Cities from London to San Francisco, from Sydney to Delhi have their Chinatown areas, where restaurants sell the food and markets sell the ingredients to avid Chinese populations as well as the locals. Chinese cooks are found all over the Indian subcontinent, Southeast Asia, country areas of Australia and New Zealand, all over the US, and in almost every country of Europe. Of all international cuisines, it is perhaps the best known, but the least tried by home cooks. I hope this book will tempt you to cook more than a simple stir-fry.

All Koreans have respect for prosperity and work hard to achieve it—in the cities, they do so in a jungle of neon. Ingenuity is a way of life and is reflected in the garlicky, sesame-scented, soya-rich sauces of the foods that these folk buy from street hawkers and traders to help them get through their hectic working day. *Bulgogi* (barbecued beef strips), *kimchee* (pickled cabbage), and rice and *kalbi chim* (beef braised with radish or chestnuts) are just three popular examples.

"Let little seem like much as long as it is fresh, natural, and beautiful" is a favorite saying in Japan. Beauty, harmony, balance, and complexity make its delicious food unique. Added to these elements are regionality, subtlety, religion, and medicine, all woven into the whole of Japanese cooking, even the street-food dishes.

Out on the street, noodles are a mainstay, just as rice is. But many street food aficionados will also be searching for beef, pork, chicken, and seafoods. Surprisingly, these days, doughnuts and hotdogs are consumed enthusiastically while, at the same time, a thousand varieties of fish and shellfish are enjoyed on a regular basis. It's one of the country's most interesting paradoxes.

The curious mix that is Japan shows itself in other ways too. Though the cola and burger phenomenon is everywhere, the Japanese still pay respects to their long-dead relatives, worship at shrines, and honor trees. But they also look forward to each year's shipment of Beaujolais Nouveau! It's a duality that they obviously enjoy, and at the same time, in Europe, America, Australia, and New Zealand, we go mad for sushi. Japanese cookery may seem intimidating, but these recipes are not. Instead I give achievable versions of some of the most delicious street dishes the country has to offer.

The ancient traditions which underpin street food in China, Japan, and Korea succeed utterly in giving it freshness, beauty, and huge taste appeal. Eating in the chaotic, busy marketplaces of these countries can be a culinary education in itself; the considered selection of perfect, fresh ingredients, their cutting, combining, and cooking over a fierce flame is a time-honored way to keep food safe to eat. Scented aromatics, sweet-salt-piquant blends, and the ever-present rice or noodles combine to give superb, nutritionally balanced dishes.

Finally, don't be afraid to mix and match. Chinese wontons can be enjoyed perfectly well before eating Japanese sushi or Korean *bulgogi* with *kimchee*. Be brave—they are all superb and will make your parties go down well with family and friends.

Top row, from left Street food breakfast in Shaoking, China. Noodles are one of the most popular street foods all over China, Korea, Japan, and all over Southeast Asia.
Center, from left Noodle bowls, ready for action. This child in China's Yunnan province has no qualms about wielding chopsticks to eat a dish of noodles, the symbol of longevity and continuity. Pork spareribs—pork and chicken are the most common meats in East and Southeast Asia.
Right Tea, in this case Japanese, originated in China, and is now the most common drink across all of Asia.

¾ cup ground pork

½ cup peeled, uncooked shrimp, deveined
  and chopped

1 inch fresh ginger, grated

4 inches daikon white radish (mooli), chopped

2 tablespoons light soy sauce

2 tablespoons chicken stock

1 tablespoon fish soy or mushroom soy

a handful of cilantro leaves, chopped

4 scallions, finely sliced

32 wonton wrappers

1 egg white, beaten

peanut oil, for deep-frying

To serve

sweet chili sauce

soy sauce

Makes 32: Serves 4

Put the pork, shrimp, ginger, daikon, soy sauce, chicken stock, fish soy, cilantro, and scallions in a food processor and work, in short bursts, to a speckled paste.

Put a small teaspoon of the mixture in the center of 1 wonton wrapper. Brush a circle of beaten egg white around the filling. Pinch and twist the wonton wrapper to enclose the filling and make a purse shape. Pull out the four corners.

Set each wonton on a dry, lightly floured board or oiled foil until all are made—they tend to stick to the surface and to each other, so keep them separate.

Fill a wok one-third full of peanut oil (or a deep-fryer to the recommended level) and heat to 300°F or until a piece of wonton skin will puff up immediately. Cook in batches of 6–8 for 2–3 minutes or until golden and crisp. Keep hot while you cook the remainder. Serve hot in small bowls or waxed paper cartons, with separate shallow dishes of the two sauces.

wontons

Hong Kong packs an amazing amount into its small area. It is a bold, beautiful, pulsing, exciting place: a mecca for shoppers and street food lovers alike. I love to explore the narrow lanes, wandering in and out of Temple Street, Ice House Street, Causeway Bay, Stanley Market, and Western Market, taking the ferry over to Kowloon late at night, or having dinner on a neon-lit giant junk. One lunchtime, at Luen Wo Market, I tasted some particularly good crispy wontons—this is my version of them.

8 oz. dried soba noodles

Dashi dipping sauce

1½ cups hot dashi stock*

¼ cup soy sauce

2 tablespoons mirin (sweet rice wine)

2 tablespoons sugar

To serve

8 scallions, finely sliced, plus the green tops,
   whole, to serve (optional)

2 teaspoons wasabi paste*

2 sheets dried nori seaweed*

1 teaspoon black sesame seeds

Serves 4

Bring a large saucepan of water to a boil, add the noodles, return to a boil, then add a cup of cold water. Return to a boil again, then add another cup of cold water. Return to a boil for a third time, then drain, refresh, and chill.

Mix the dipping sauce ingredients in a bowl, then divide between 4 soup-style bowls. Put the scallions in 4 side bowls, with ½ teaspoon of wasabi paste beside.

Take the nori sheets, one by one, in a pair of tongs and wave over a low gas flame or hot element until they smell toasty and feel crisp. Crumble or cut into shreds. Divide the noodles between the 4 soup bowls, sprinkle with sesame seeds, add the nori, and serve with scallion tops, if using.

soba noodles

Chilled Japanese Buckwheat Noodles

From one end of Japan to the other, you'll see diners bending intently over bowls of these cold buckwheat noodles—at noodle shops, bars, and corner cafés in every town and city throughout the country, but especially in the north, where they originated. Noodle bars are often found near train and bus stations and are one of Japan's gifts to an appreciative world. Soba noodle bars are now proliferating widely, and you'll find them from Sydney to Seattle, from Salzburg to Singapore. For the correct ingredients go to a Japanese grocer or specialty Asian food store: instant dashi is sold in different forms (see note), and you can also make your own using dried kombu seaweed and bonito flakes.

■ **note:** Dashi stock is sold in powder or concentrate form in Asian stores and large supermarkets. If difficult to find, use chicken stock instead. Wasabi paste is hot Japanese horseradish, also sold in supermarkets, as is dried nori seaweed.

8 oz. uncooked jumbo shrimp,

8 oz. squid caps, opened out flat

8 fresh shiitake

3 oz. enokitake mushrooms (optional)

8 parsley sprigs with stalks

8 perilla, arugula, or spinach leaves

flour, for dusting

peanut oil, for frying

Dipping sauce

1 cup dashi (see note, page 116) or chicken stock

¼ cup light soy sauce

2 tablespoons mirin (sweet rice wine) or dry sherry

1 tablespoon sugar

2 tablespoons grated or sliced fresh ginger

4 inches daikon white radish (mooli), grated

1 fresh red chili, finely chopped

Tempura batter

1 egg yolk

¾ cup sifted all-purpose flour

Serves 4

Tempura—probably invented between 1550 and 1650 AD in Nagasaki, not by the Japanese but by homesick Portuguese or Spaniards—is a delicious dish in which a selection of food is covered with a light, lacy, airy batter and fried quickly, then served with a dipping sauce. It's now found all around the world and is perfect takeout food.

The batter should be barely mixed: make half at a time, then mix a second batch for a crisp, fresh effect. Shrimp and squid, as used here, taste and look good: add greens to balance the flavors. If you can't find perilla (shiso) leaves, use arugula or baby spinach. Have all the fish and seafood prepared, the dip made, the chili-daikon mixture ready, the oil hot, and make and use the batter at the very end. This egg-yolk tempura is the one preferred in Osaka— pale yellow, not white. In Tokyo, it's often used with egg white and is much paler.

Peel and devein the shrimp and score them several times on the underside to prevent them from curling. Cut the squid into even 2-inch squares and score them, criss-cross, on both sides. Halve the shiitakes and trim the enokitake. Assemble all the ingredients to be fried and dust them with flour.

To make the dipping sauce, mix the dashi or stock, soy, mirin, sugar, and ginger together.

Mix the grated daikon and chopped chili in a small bowl.

Fill a wok or saucepan one-third full of oil and heat to 350°F or until a noodle fluffs up immediately.

To make the batter, put the egg yolk into a bowl, add ½ cup ice water and beat 2–3 times only. Add the sifted flour, mix again, minimally, until barely mixed and lumpy-looking. Using chopsticks, dip each piece into the batter, then cook in the hot oil. Do not cook more than 5 pieces at once or the temperature will drop. Remove each batch and keep hot while you cook the remainder.

Serve with a pile of the chili-daikon mixture and a bowl of the dipping sauce.

tempura

Crispy Japanese Seafood and Leaves

Barbecuing is one of the most typical Korean cooking methods. On Sundays, all over Seoul—indeed over much of Korea—you'll see families at outdoor restaurants preparing *bulgogi* and *kalbi chim* (glazed char-grilled spareribs), the two favorite local street foods. *Bulgogi* is finely sliced marinated beef, briefly flashed on both sides over a heated metal surface. Crisp leaves are filled with the beef, fruit, and *kimchee*, Korea's famous chili-powered pickle, then rolled up and eaten with the fingers.

bulgogi

Korean Barbecued Beef

3 lb. beef tenderloin, finely sliced teriyaki-style

Barbecue marinade

½ cup dark soy sauce

¼ cup sugar

3 garlic cloves, finely chopped

4 scallions, finely chopped

1 inch fresh ginger, grated

2 tablespoons sesame oil

2 tablespoons toasted sesame seeds

To serve

1 cup *kimchee* pickle (Korean cabbage)

30 crisp lettuce leaves

2 Asian pears (nashi), crisp apples, or nectarines,

   cut in wedges

8 scallions, cut in strips lengthwise

2 tablespoons toasted sesame seeds

Serves 6

Put all the marinade ingredients into a shallow bowl, add the beef slices, and turn until well coated. Chill for 30 minutes.

Assemble all the serving accompaniments in separate bowls before cooking.

Heat a *bulgogi* pan, stove-top grill pan, or skillet until very hot. Using tongs, add the beef slices, one at a time, to the hot surface. Let cook until aromatic, then turn and cook the other side. (The outside should be caramelized and the insides succulent and tender, but cook it longer if you prefer.)

Each person takes a lettuce leaf, adds a piece of beef, quartered if necessary, and their choice of *kimchee*, pears, scallions, and sesame seeds.

1 plump duck, about 3 lb., cleaned and prepared

1 teaspoon five-spice powder

2 teaspoons salt

2 tablespoons Chinese oyster sauce

peanut oil, for deep-frying

Glaze

2 tablespoons light corn syrup

2 teaspoons distilled white vinegar

2 teaspoons sake or vodka

To serve

2 lb. cooked rice or 16 Peking duck pancakes

8 inches cucumber, in 2-inch strips

8 scallions, finely sliced lengthwise

1 cup plum sauce or hoisin sauce

Serves 4

Wash the duck well and pat dry with paper towels. Mix the five-spice, salt, and oyster sauce in a bowl and rub it all over the inside of the bird. Tie the neck and neck skin with string so the duck can be hung up. Put the duck in a colander and pour boiling water over it 5 times, drying off the bird between each pouring. Pat dry again.

Put the glaze ingredients and ½ cup water into a small saucepan, bring to a boil, and cook until sticky, about 10 minutes. Using a small brush, paint the glaze all over the duck. Hang up the bird by the string in a hot, breezy place, or in front of a hair dryer or electric fan, until it is completely dry.

Fill a large wok or skillet one-third full of peanut oil and immerse the duck. Heat the oil to 360°F or until a piece of bread browns in 40 seconds. Deep-fry the duck for 30 minutes, then turn with tongs and fry for a further 30 minutes.

Alternatively, preheat the oven to 375°F. Put the duck on its back on a rack in a roasting pan and roast for 45 minutes. Reduce to 300°F, turn the duck onto its breast, and roast for 30 minutes. Increase the heat to 375°F, turn the duck over again, and roast for 30 minutes.

To serve, slice the duck, including skin, meat, and bone, into ½-inch slices with a Chinese cleaver. Transfer, in sections, to a serving plate. Serve hot with rice or pancakes, cucumber, scallions, and sauce.

peking duck

A famous and princely dish, sold in restaurants and street-side eateries in Asia and in Chinatowns around the world. Though easily available these days ready-made from many Chinese restaurants, it is fascinating to know how to make the duck yourself. A hair dryer or electric fan is useful if you do not live in a place with a hot, dry, windy climate (in other words, most of us). Usually served with pancakes and garnishes, the duck is also excellent with plain rice. Try it, adding the cucumber, scallions, and plum sauce as accompaniments.

bento boxes

Japanese Lunch Boxes

1 cup sushi rice or short-grain rice

2-inch piece dried kombu (Japanese kelp)

3 tablespoons clear rice vinegar

3 tablespoons sugar

2 inches fresh ginger, grated (optional)

2 garlic cloves, finely chopped (optional)

1 teaspoon salt

½ daikon radish (mooli), sliced wafer-thin

1 carrot, sliced wafer-thin

4 sheets dried nori seaweed, cut in 1-inch strips
   or 2-inch squares

4 oz. salmon, tuna, or mackerel, sushi-grade if
   possible, cut in 16 thin slices, or smoked salmon

2 tablespoons teriyaki glaze (optional)

Your choice of:

chives, black sesame seeds, finely sliced scallions,
   smoked salmon, peeled shrimp, smoked eel, or
   fruit such as cherries or sliced pear

To serve

Japanese pickled ginger

green wasabi paste

puréed ginger paste

Japanese soy sauce

Serves 4

At bus and train stations all over Japan, bento boxes are the ultimate in street food chic! These wooden lunchboxes (or lacquered plastic or cardboard versions, these days) contain rice and delicious treats such as meatballs, clams, sour plums, salmon, eel, scallions, and sushi—a different combination in each region, though the plum is almost always included because it gives the dish prized astringency. Condiments are enclosed in little dishes. Sparklingly fresh raw fish is a traditional ingredient in these recipes, but many westerners prefer it smoked or cooked with a teriyaki glaze. All the serving accompaniments are sold ready-made in bottles or tubes in Asian stores and many supermarkets.

Put the rice into a sieve, wash well, and soak in cold running water for a few minutes, kneading gently until the water runs clear. Drain well, then put the rice and kombu into a saucepan. Add 1 cup boiling water, return to a boil, cover, reduce to a gentle simmer, and cook for 8 minutes. Turn off the heat and let stand for another 8 minutes.

Dissolve the sugar and vinegar in a small pitcher. Transfer the rice to a shallow dish, then fan it with one hand while you drizzle over the sweet vinegar with the other. Stir, then add the ginger and garlic if using (unorthodox but delicious). Cover and let cool.

Divide the rice into 4, then divide again to make 32 pieces. Shape each one into cubes, rectangles or rounds. Leave some plain and decorate others.

Suggestions include: wrapping the rice in daikon or cucumber that has been finely sliced with a vegetable peeler, then adding finely sliced carrot above and below; wrapping in nori strips, squares, or cones, then topping with fish—raw, smoked, or brushed with teriyaki glaze; or adding your choice of other garnishes or pickled ginger.

Arrange the sushi on small white plates. Alternatively, for a party, serve them in individual shallow Japanese bento boxes (from specialty Japanese and other Asian shops), rectangular plastic lidded boxes, or even on disposable plates. Add small dishes of wasabi paste, soy sauce, and Japanese pink pickled ginger as accompaniments.

Street food down under, like its people, boasts an eclectic cultural mix. British colonial traditions have

been overlaid with waves of immigration from mainland Europe, especially the Mediterranean, as well

as the Middle East, South America, China, and Southeast Asia. The result is a vibrant, exciting food

culture and a population willing to try anything in culinary terms.

australia
and new zealand

Australia and New Zealand are exciting places for gastronomy in general and street food in particular. The first Europeans to settle in both countries were British, but after World War II, people from all over Europe settled in Australia. From the 1970s, more settlers arrived in Australia from Southeast Asia, South America, and the Middle East, all of whom had an exciting and beneficial effect on food culture. Australia is more polyglot, more Mediterranean and Asian in its cuisine than New Zealand, but both countries reflect the diverse nature of their immigrants. Exchange between New Zealand and Australia is important, though there has always been a certain rivalry, as between cousins or brothers and sisters. Young Australians and New Zealanders flock abroad for what is referred to as "overseas experience"—backpacking around the world. They start in the cafés and harborside restaurants of Sydney or Auckland before venturing further north to California, the east coast of America, and then to Europe. Frequently they work their way around the world for several years—often in restaurants, bars, or cafés—before heading home. On their return they bring with them Asian food accents, European cooking ideas, Mediterranean verve, American excitement, and a magpie-like eclecticism.

"New Australians" of Italian, Greek, Lebanese, Chinese, and Southeast Asian descent have produced miracles in downtown restaurants, suburban and country eateries, and outdoor food stalls and kiosks. Specialty traders import and export foodstuffs all over the globe. The produce—fish, fruits, nuts, herbs, spices, vegetables, specially-bred livestock, and imported exotics—offer an eye-popping choice to the cooking, street-food-snacking, and restaurant-going public.

The large cities of both countries are now thoroughly cosmopolitan. Once, you could only find traditional street foods ranging from hamburgers to *chow mein*, fish and chips to Chinese spring rolls. These days the bustling, fashionable markets sell fresh or cooked food from around the world. You can buy local versions of Indonesian *nasi goreng*, Malaysian *laksa*, Korean *bulgogi*, Chinese dim sum, or noodles, Vietnamese *pho bo*, *loempia* from the Philippines, and samosas or tandoori from India—not to mention chocolate cakes from Vienna, coffee from Greece, and gelati from Italy.

In New Zealand particularly, the Pacific-island influence is also important, and you will find raw fish in coconut milk, banana desserts from the Cook Islands, or Maori rewena (potato) bread.

Fish and seafood are some of the most important ingredients sold as street food, restaurant fare, and in home cooking. You can buy crayfish live or newly boiled from New Zealand roadside stalls. Local shellfish such as *paua* (abalone), *pipis,* and *tuatuas* are made into batter-covered patties, ground into cakes, or used for soup. Oysters are enormously popular, especially the strongly flavored New Zealand Bluff oysters, dainty Sydney rock oysters, and larger ones from all along the east coast. Freshly-cooked shrimp are a traditional takeout, simply sprinkled with salt and lemon, then wrapped in paper to be shelled and eaten on the beach, in the "bush" (country), or at home.

But what to drink? Once, the alcohol of choice in Australia and New Zealand would have been beer (and sometimes still is). Today, their wine industries are the envy of the world, and the fresh varietal wines are perfectly suited to the outdoor lifestyles of both countries.

Top right Typical Australian fusion food—an eclectic mix of cultures in a spicy Thai-style version of British fish and chips. *Clockwise from below* Australia and New Zealand grow fruits and vegetables from around the world: these are cooking bananas or plantains. The coffee bars of Melbourne's Acland Street, St. Kilda, are famous for wonderful coffee and cakes introduced by immigrants from Central Europe. Seafood, especially shrimp, is inexpensive and plentiful—ubiquitous fare in restaurants and street food cafés. Steinlager from New Zealand is one of the many beer brands that have migrated around the world from the Antipodes. Fresh fruit drinks, such as the smoothie, are sold from juice bars in markets and on beachfronts all around the Australian coast: this one is based on the Peach Melba, a sinfully rich dessert created by Escoffier for the famous Australian opera singer, Dame Nellie Melba. It includes peaches and raspberries.

pork dim sum

with Sweet Soy Sauce

60–75 wonton skins

Pork filling

1 lb. ground pork

8 scallions, chopped

6 tablespoons soy sauce

3 tablespoons sesame oil

2 tablespoons grated fresh ginger

4 oz. bok choy, spring cabbage, or spinach, sliced

Sweet soy sauce

1 tablespoon soy sauce

2 tablespoons balsamic vinegar

2 tablespoons clear honey or sugar

2 scallions, finely sliced

1 teaspoon sliced red chili

⅓ cup boiling stock or water

Makes 60–70: Serves 12

The Chinese were some of the earliest immigrants to Australia, arriving during the gold rush period of the mid-nineteenth century. These days, all the state capitals have Chinatown areas, but the biggest and most exciting is in Sydney's Haymarket—street after street of wonderful shops and restaurants, and a buzzing open-air life.
There's an underground life too—a huge open area under Chinatown, crammed with takeout food bars and cafés, where dishes like this are sold. These delicate steamed dumplings are a down-under version of the classic poached water dumplings, usually made at Chinese New Year. Use wonton skins or wrappers—easy to locate in any Chinatown—and shape the dumplings into half moons, "hat" shapes, or both.
Serve them for a party in carryout containers with paper to separate the layers, little plastic cups for the sauce, and disposable chopsticks, echoing their street origins.

Put the pork filling ingredients in a food processor and mix them together in brief bursts. Alternatively, mix in a bowl, using your hands.

To make half-moon dumplings, scissor-cut the wrappers into circles and discard the trimmings. Put 1 teaspoon of filling in the center of each circle. Wet all the edges and fold the wrapper in half. Pinch closed the top of the curved edges, pleat the sides in 2 places, and press firmly to seal. Gently push downward so the dumplings sit flat with the curved seam on top. Put on a dry, floured surface while you make the remaining dumplings.

To make hat-shaped dumplings, put 1 teaspoon of filling in the center of each square wonton skin. Wet all the edges, pinch the 2 diagonal points together, then into a high peak. Seal the long edges, wet the 2 tail points, overlap them in front, then pinch closed.

Put the dumplings in a bamboo or metal steamer set over a wok or saucepan of boiling water and steam for 6 minutes or until cooked and translucent.

Mix all ingredients for the sweet soy sauce together in a bowl and serve with the dumplings.

white

bait and kumara

Whitebait Fritters and Kumara Chips

6 tablespoons all-purpose flour or fresh

   breadcrumbs

3 eggs, beaten

4 sprigs of parsley, chopped

1½ cups New Zealand whitebait or other very

   small fish such as elvers

sea salt and freshly ground black pepper

virgin olive oil, for frying

lemon wedges, to serve

Kumara chips

2 lb. kumara or other orange sweet potatoes, cut

   into ribbon-like strips with a vegetable peeler

cayenne pepper

sea salt flakes

virgin olive oil, for frying

Serves 6

New Zealand whitebait are the miniature offspring of the inunga fish. They taste delicately sweet-but-salty. Cooked, they look like short lengths of white pasta dotted with silver. They are nothing like European whitebait, which are small, silvery fish like miniature sardines, or the American variety, a kind of smelt, that grows up to 8 inches long. Any tiny fish, or elvers, are possible substitutes. Once, whitebait were common, but now, like many good things, they are seasonal, rather rare and expensive and therefore a special treat. These days, they are worthy of serving with one of the best New Zealand wines, perhaps a precious bottle of Cloudy Bay sauvignon blanc.

Kumara can be made into fries, like ordinary french fries, but I have cut them into transparent ribbons and deep-fried them into chips; use the common orange sweet potato if you can't find genuine New Zealand kumara.

To make the chips, fill a saucepan or deep-fryer one-third full of olive oil (or to the manufacturer's recommended level) and heat to 375°F, or until a cube of bread browns in 30 seconds.

Pat the kumara dry with paper towels, then put into a frying basket and cook, one basket at a time, without crowding the strips. Fry for 6–8 minutes, shaking the basket from time to time. Remove, drain, and keep hot while you cook the remainder. Sprinkle with cayenne and sea salt.

Meanwhile, put the flour or breadcrumbs, eggs, salt, and black pepper into a bowl and beat well. Stir in the parsley. Drop in the whitebait and stir them gently to mix—there should be barely enough batter to keep the little fish together.

Heat about ½-inch depth of oil in a heavy-bottomed skillet. Drop in a large, heaping tablespoon of the mixture and press flat to form a disk about 2 inches in diameter. Cook for 1–2 minutes per side. Remove, keep hot, and repeat until all the mixture has been used. Serve immediately with lemon wedges and kumara chips.

■ **note:** Though whitebait have moved from the everyday to the special occasion, kumara chips make perfect party food (make lots, people love them!)

vietnamese pork

Pork Brochettes with Nuóc Cham Dipping Sauce

1 lb. pork tenderloin or 4 large, boneless pork

    chops, cut into ½-inch cubes

4 garlic cloves, chopped

2 tablespoons fish sauce

1 tablespoon fresh lime juice

2 tablespoons sugar

6 kaffir lime leaves, sliced hair-thin

8 inches fresh lemongrass, finely sliced (3–4 stalks)

2 inches fresh ginger, finely sliced

1 small hot bird's eye chili, sliced

Nuóc cham dipping sauce

1 teaspoon sugar

1 tablespoon fresh lime juice

3 tablespoons fish sauce

1 red or green chili, sliced

2 inches scallion green, finely sliced

Table salad

16 lettuce leaves

8 oz. cooked rice noodles or beanthread noodles

1 carrot, finely sliced

your choice of: mint, basil, cilantro, flat-leaf

    parsley, garlic chives, beansprouts, or cucumber

Serves 4

This Vietnamese recipe, one of the many introduced by recent immigrants from Vietnam, has been comfortably absorbed into Antipodean street food culture. It is vividly pungent—superb when combined with with noodles and fragrant herbs and salad leaves. In Vietnam as well as Australia, the choice of ingredients in the "table salad" would be huge, but use whatever Asian-style herbs and salad leaves you have available. *Nuóc cham* is the fresh-tasting dipping sauce served with many Vietnamese dishes.

Put the garlic, fish sauce, lime juice, and sugar in a shallow non-metal dish and stir. Stir in the lime leaves, lemongrass, ginger, and chili. Add the pork, stir, and set aside to marinate for 20 minutes. Meanwhile, soak 12 short satay sticks in water for 30 minutes, then drain and push 6–7 pieces of pork onto each satay stick.

Heat a cast-iron stove-top grill pan or non-stick skillet and press the satays onto the hot surface, turning until browned all over and cooked right through, about 4 minutes. Remove the satays and keep them warm. Add any remaining marinade and boil briefly until reduced to form a glaze. Meanwhile put the dipping sauce ingredients in a small bowl and stir well.

Arrange the table salad ingredients on a serving platter, and divide the satays between 4 small plates. To eat, pull the meat off the sticks. Take a lettuce leaf, add a tangle of noodles and carrots, then the meat and your choice of table salad ingredients. Roll up the leaf to form a parcel, dip it into the *nuóc cham*, then eat with your fingers.

■ **note:** Use scissors, a razor blade, or pen knife to slice kaffir lime leaves (also known as *makrut*) into hair-fine slices; any thicker and they become indigestible and difficult to eat.

satays

lebanese

"New Australians," as immigrants are called in Australia, have contributed greatly to the color, vitality, and cultural and gastronomic life of the country. This Australian-Lebanese dish, rather like Greek *souvlaki*, but using lamb carved from one whole, tender, barbecued chunk of mid-loin fillet, is utterly delicious and easy to make. Lamb is delectable and economical in a country of many millions of sheep, but you could also use other cuts of lamb, or even chicken. Buy ready-made hummus and tabbouleh from a delicatessen or supermarket, or make your own. Use flatbreads such as *lavash* or large, soft pita bread to wrap around the filling. This is a takeout lunch treat, so tropical fruit juice would be a perfect drink—or, for a late-night snack, try a very cold Australian beer or berry-scented Shiraz (Syrah).

souvlaki

Lamb, Tabbouleh, and Hummus in Flatbread

4 garlic cloves, crushed

juice of ½ lemon

1 teaspoon cumin seeds, toasted in a dry skillet,
    then ground

1 teaspoon freshly ground black pepper

2 tablespoons extra-virgin olive oil

one 2½ lb. lamb loin roast, trimmed of fat
    and boned

salt and freshly ground black pepper

To serve

1 cup hummus

1 cup tabbouleh salad

6 soft Middle Eastern flatbreads,
    such as *lavash* or pita

harissa or other hot chili sauce, to serve (optional)

Serves 6

Put the garlic, lemon juice, cumin, pepper, and oil in a shallow bowl, add the lamb, turn to coat, and leave for 20 minutes to 2 hours. Heat a stove-top grill pan, broiler, or barbecue and cook the lamb gently so the outside is dark and smoky but the inside still rosy, about 20 minutes. Remove and set aside in a warm place, covered, for 5 minutes, then slice diagonally. Sprinkle with salt. Add the marinade ingredients to the grill pan or a saucepan, bring to a boil, then trickle it over the meat. Warm the breads briefly over the coals or under the broiler. Spoon a line of hummus down the middle, top with a good layer of tabbouleh, then top with the sliced lamb. Drizzle with the lamb juices, and season to taste. Add a trickle of chili sauce, if using.

Roll up the bread, tucking one end over if using *lavash*, then wrap tightly in a double layer of butcher's paper to stop the juices running out, folding up the end, to form a tight tube with the top of the *souvlaki* open at the other end.

■ **note:** To make your own tabbouleh, soak 4 oz. plain bulgar wheat in water for 20 minutes, then drain. Chop 2 large tomatoes, 3 scallions, a large bunch of parsley, and another of mint. Put all the ingredients in a bowl with ¼ cup olive oil and 2 tablespoon lemon juice. Sprinkle with salt and pepper and toss well.

baklava

Greek Honey-Nut Sticky Pastries

18 sheets phyllo pastry, about 10 oz.

generous ¾ cup butter, melted, plus extra

   for greasing

2 cups chopped macadamia nuts, walnuts, or

   pistachios

1 cup chopped blanched almonds

¼ cup sugar

2 teaspoons ground cinnamon

a pinch of ground cloves

Honey syrup

1 cup sugar

3 tablespoons flower-scented honey, such as

   Tasmanian leatherwood

2 cinnamon sticks, crushed

zest, cut in 1 strip, and juice of 1 lemon

Makes 30 pieces: Serves 8

■ **note:** Keep phyllo pastry under a damp cloth
while you work, to keep it supple.

Butter the base and sides of a baking dish, 14 x 8 x 2 inches. Place 9 sheets of phyllo (about 5 oz.) in the base, buttering each one. Preheat the oven to 325°F.

Put the nuts, sugar, cinnamon, and cloves into a food processor and work in short bursts to a coarse meal. Spread over the pastry sheets, pushing it down evenly.

Continue layering with the remaining pastry and butter. Using a thin, sharp blade, such as a razor blade or pen knife, cut even, diagonal, diamond shapes through the top few layers.

Bake in the center of the oven for 30 minutes. Transfer to the top shelf of the oven and cook for a further 30 minutes, covering loosely with baking parchment or foil if it is browning to much.

Mix the syrup ingredients together with 1 cup boiling water, and crush the zest to release the flavors. Stir over a moderate heat, uncovered, for 12 minutes. Let cool. Alternatively, microwave on HIGH for 4 minutes, covered, then 2 minutes, uncovered.

When the baklava is cooked, drizzle syrup evenly over the top of the pastry, then let cool for 2 hours. Cut and serve or transfer to an airtight container within 2 hours, before the pastry loses its crispness. It will keep for 2–3 weeks.

Australian Greeks have contributed hugely to the food scene in Australia. In fact Melbourne, capital of the state of Victoria, is said to be the second biggest Greek city in the world. Sticky pastries are a passion with Greeks, and they are equally popular with all Australians. Even people who don't like sweet things give in when they taste one of these. A *glikha* (sweet, strong, Greek coffee) and a glass of ice-cold water are perfect accompaniments. Sweetmeats like these, made with almonds and pistachios, are found all over the Balkans and the Middle East and are of ancient lineage. This version uses macadamia nuts, native to the rainforests of Queensland, Australia, and honey made from the blossoms of the Tasmanian leatherwood tree (use any highly-scented honey if you can't find leatherwood).

Every summer, when just like the swallows I return to New Zealand, I have various homecoming rituals. A favorite is eating a cone of hokey pokey as I walk down sunny streets. New Zealand's dairy products are superb so, unlike in some parts of the world, its ice cream does actually taste of milk and cream as it should, with an appealing, clean, honest simplicity. Sadly, hokey pokey in England, in the distant past, used to be a coded reference to poor quality. Conversely, in Scotland, it was a contraction of the words *"ecco poco,"* the cry of Italian ice cream vendors there, meaning "Here's a little treat!" The toffee component of New Zealand's hokey pokey is known as honeycomb toffee or cinder in other parts of the world. You must make this first and cool it before beginning the ice cream. It is smashed to bits and added after churning.

hokey pokey

Honeycomb Toffee Ice Cream

6 egg yolks

1 cup sugar

2½ cups heavy cream

2½ cups milk, very cold

2 teaspoons vanilla extract

Hokey pokey

¼ cup sugar

2 tablespoons corn syrup

1 teaspoon baking soda

butter, for greasing

Serves 6

To make the hokey pokey, first butter a shallow metal pan. Mix the sugar and syrup in a saucepan and bring to a boil, stirring. Continue boiling, stirring occasionally, for 4½ –5 minutes or until a candy thermometer registers 285°F.

Stir in the baking soda—the mixture will foam immediately. Stir quickly, pour into the prepared pan, then let cool and set.

When set, put into a plastic bag and smash into ½-inch pieces.

To make the ice cream, beat the egg yolks and sugar in a heatproof bowl. Pour the cream into a small saucepan, heat to boiling point, then pour it onto the egg yolks, beating constantly. Cool over ice water, then stir in the milk and vanilla.

Churn in an ice cream maker for 20–30 minutes or until set. Remove, mix with the hokey pokey, and pack into a freezer-proof container. Cover, label, and fast-freeze for at least 1 hour, or until hard. Alternatively, freeze in plastic trays until the mixture is hard at the edges but soft in the center. Remove and stir well, then refreeze as before. Repeat and refreeze. Serve in dishes, cones, or between wafers.

pacific poke

Banana-Coconut Dessert

1 cup sugar

7–8 ripe bananas, mashed, about 2 lb.

¾ cup milk

½ cup arrowroot

1½ cups canned coconut milk, plus extra to serve

confectioners' sugar, for dusting

Serves 4

Poke (it rhymes with okay) is not the world's most elegant dessert. In fact its odd appearance almost discouraged me from trying it at Auckland's Otara market, a place crammed with Pacific-Asian products. Cook Island women were selling gaudy hats, beaded pitcher covers, shell-trimmed table mats, and infant christening dresses and there—lurking in the middle of the colorful jumble—were some containers of poke. They gave me some to taste, and I was smitten! It is curiously delicious: the banana is almost caramelized, the rest jelly-like. This is a true taste of the South Pacific!

Put the sugar into a 10-inch heavy-bottomed stainless steel or non-stick skillet. Add ¾ cup boiling water and heat gently until the sugar has dissolved. Stir in a layer of mashed bananas and cook over moderate heat until it begins to stick and turn dark and slightly pink. Every 8 minutes or so, scrape the thick paste off the base with a wooden spatula and continue cooking until a new layer begins to stick. Continue this process until the banana turns a rich, darkish color and is reduced to about 1 cup, about 50 minutes. Cool slightly.

Preheat the oven to 350°F. Beat the milk and arrowroot in a bowl, until smooth. Stir the mixture into the banana, then transfer to a lightly oiled, round 7-inch ovenproof dish, about 1 inch deep. Bake uncovered for 1–1¼ hours, or until set.

Pierce all over with a fork or skewer, then pour over the well-stirred coconut milk. Return the poke to the oven for 20 minutes and turn off the heat. Leave for 30 minutes, then remove from the oven. Let cool a little, then cut into wedges and serve cool or cold, dusted with confectioners' sugar, and drizzled with a little extra coconut milk.

index

photographic credits

■ Jacket Tony Stone Images, Neil Beer
■ Adams Picture Library, Malcolm
& Yoko Fairman p 7, 2nd row left
■ Cephas p 7, 1st row center/
pp 110–111
■ Greg Evans International
Photography p 7, 3rd row center/
p 39, 3rd row left/94–95/pp 126–127
■ Oona van den Berg p 96, 3rd row
right
■ Panos Pictures, Paul Smith p 11,
3rd row center/Jeremy Hartley p 62,
3rd row right/Wang Gang Feng p 113,
1st row left
■ Peter Hince pp 60–61
■ The Photographers Library p 7, 1st
row right, 2nd row center/ p 11, 1st
row center
■ Robert Harding Picture Library,
Adam Woolfitt p 39, 1st row right/
Nik Wheeler p 39, 3rd row right/JHC
Wilson p 81, 3rd row right
■ Tony Stone Images, Paul Harris
p 7, 2nd row right/Joseph Sohm
pp 12–13/Greg Pease p 15, top/Paul
Harris p 11, 2nd row center/Steven
Rothfeld pp 36–37/Nicholas DeVore
pp 78–79/Dale Boyer p 96, top right/
Glen Allison p 96, 2nd row center/
Yann Layma p 113, 2nd row center
■ The Stock Market Photo Agency
Inc. p 11, 2nd row left
■ Sylvia Cordaiy Photo Library,
Graeme Goldin p 81, 2nd row center